Dis

Historic
Wavertree

Village and Garden Suburb

by Mike Chitty

Published by The Wavertree Society

First published in 1999 by
The Wavertree Society,
P.O.Box 100, Wavertree,
Liverpool L15 5DQ.

ISBN 0 9536441 0 3

Printed by Printfine Limited, Liverpool.

Publication of this book was assisted by grants from Barclays
Bank of Wavertree Technology Park, Liverpool L69 2LN,
and from ABSA: the Association for Business Sponsorship of
the Arts

ACKNOWLEDGEMENTS

This book has been many years in the making. I have a lot of people to thank, both for supplying information and for getting the results into print. It was the late John Maw who, in May 1977, gave a talk on 'Old Wavertree' to the pre-inaugural meeting of the Wavertree Society, and inspired me - a newcomer to the area - to lead the first of several Walkabouts a few months later. The object of these walks was to gather, not just to give out, information, and many of those who attended have been unwitting contributors to this publication.

Individuals such as Joan Borrowscale and the late Eddie Barker have supplied me with numerous historical snippets arising from their own researches. I have, over the years, received letters from all over the country - and, indeed, abroad - from people researching their families' Wavertree roots, and they too have supplied me with material which has been of great interest and use. Others have written down their reminiscences of Wavertree places and people. I would particularly like to thank Mrs L. Collins for her account of the life of Charles Berrington, based on the memories of Mrs Ada Kolb.

The book's appearance in print is largely due to the efforts of successive Chairmen of the Wavertree Society - Joyce Edwards, Robert Zatz and John Wood - who have kept up the pressure on me to put pen to paper and, latterly, fingers to keyboard. Various Committee members of the Society have helped by walking the route, draft text in hand, doing their best to spot mistakes in the directions. Any errors which remain, however, are entirely my responsibility.

My thanks go to Dai Gwynne for his excellent line drawings (pages 19, 20, 32, 38, 41, 47, 54, 56, 59, 62,

69, 71, 75, 84 and 95), to Charlie Keith for the sketch of Rose Cottage on page 21, to Mrs M. Kavanagh for the use of the Sandown Lane photograph (page 26) and to Florence Gersten for the loan of several old postcards. The maps and pictures on pages 2, 5, 9, 17, 34, 45, 82 and 92 are reproduced with the permission of the Liverpool Libraries and Information Services. The staff of the Liverpool Record Office and Local Studies Library have also been helpful in many other ways.

Both I and the Society are, of course, especially grateful to Barclays Bank on the Wavertree Technology Park, whose generosity has allowed the printer to be paid. The grant from their Community Projects Fund has also paved the way for a series of plaques and display boards within Wavertree's two Conservation Areas.

Last, but not least, I must thank my wife Eryl (Wavertree-born) and my son Martin (currently a pupil at the Blue Coat School) for their tolerance while I have been out and about researching this book, or busy at home on the computer!

Mike Chitty
June 1999

ABOUT THE AUTHOR

Mike Chitty was born in London in 1949. He has lived in Liverpool since 1973, and was a resident of Wavertree Garden Suburb between 1975 and 1982. Having been Honorary Secretary of the Wavertree Society from 1977 until 1982, he is now the Society's Local History and Conservation Secretary. As a Merseyside Blue Badge tourist guide since 1980, he has led walks and tours, and given talks, on a variety of themes relating to Liverpool past, present and future.

CONTENTS

Fold-out maps of the route are included after pages
68 and 92, as follows:

LIST OF ILLUSTRATIONS

INTRODUCTION

Wavertree is a village in the city. Though situated only three miles from the centre of Liverpool, and though it has been administered by the City Council since 1895, Wavertree is still recognisable as a much older settlement than the suburbs which surround it.

In fact - unlike Liverpool, which did not exist at all prior to 1207 - Wavertree can be said to be as old as any place in the country for which records survive. It was an Anglo-Saxon manor, and in the Domesday Book it is recorded: "Leving held Wauretreu. There are 2 carucates of land. It was worth 64 pence". Going back even further, it can claim to be one of the oldest settlements in the whole of Merseyside, for Bronze Age burial urns have been unearthed in North Drive, Victoria Park.

The name was, in the past, variously spelt Watry, Wartre, Waurtree and Wavertree. It was always called "Wa'tree" by the locals, until 'educated' newcomers in the nineteenth century insisted on pronouncing the name in accordance with the (by then) official spelling. Scholars have argued over the meaning of the name: some claiming it refers to 'a wavering tree', some preferring 'a clearing in a wood', and others 'the place by the common pond'.

Whatever the derivation of the name, it was almost certainly the availability of a water supply which encouraged the growth of the original agricultural settlement. The earliest maps, dating from the eighteenth century, show that the focal point of the village was the road junction where the Picton Clock now stands. There was a cluster of buildings in Mill Lane, close to the ancient township well. Other buildings straggled along the present-day Church Road North, High Street and Prince Alfred Road (then called 'Cow Lane'). The road from Liverpool - now called Picton Road, but originally 'Wavertree Lane' - was little more than a muddy trackway, until the remarkable growth of the port in the eighteenth century made communication between Wavertree and its neighbour more important.

Historically, Wavertree was a Township in the parish of Childwall, in the hundred of West Derby, in the county of Lancashire. Its boundaries followed Binns Road in the north, Priory Road (now Queens Drive) and Gipsy Lane in the east, Rose Lane in the south, and Spofforth Road in the west. The population of the Township grew rapidly during the nineteenth century: from just 860 in 1801 to 4,000 in 1851 and 25,000 by 1901.

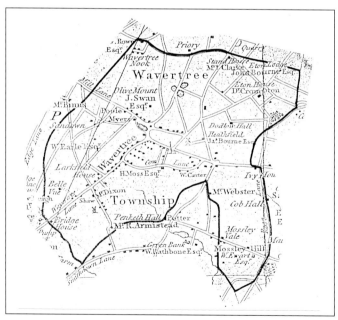

[An extract from James Sherriff's 'Map of the environs of Liverpool', 1826, showing the boundaries of the Township of Wavertree]

Much of this growth was a direct consequence of the expansion of Liverpool. Initially, it was the wealthy merchants and others, with business interests in the town, who chose to move out into the countryside and into villages such as Wavertree. Later on, particularly after the introduction of cheap and frequent tram services along the main radial routes, it was the clerks, the managers and the artisans who moved out into the new and ever-expanding suburban housing areas.

By the end of the nineteenth century, Wavertree had almost - but not quite - been overrun by the city of Liverpool. The tide of new housing had reached Wellington Road and Rathbone Road. But there was concern about the social consequences of this expansion. In 1895 an anonymous benefactor had presented Wavertree Playground to the people of the city, as a rare green open space where children could enjoy healthy recreation. In 1910 Wavertree Nook became the site of one of England's first Garden Suburbs, designed to prove that trees and greenery were not incompatible with 'ordinary' people's rented housing in a city like Liverpool.

So it was that Wavertree escaped obliteration, and survives today as a uniquely varied and interesting part of Liverpool. Wavertree has a greater density of Listed Buildings (of Architectural and Historic Interest) than almost any other district of the city. The Garden Suburb has been a Conservation Area since 1971, and Wavertree Village since 1979.

The history of Wavertree since the eighteenth century is a reflection of the history of Liverpool, and one of the best ways of discovering that history is to take a walk along its streets. The object of this book is to guide you on that journey. It will take you back to prehistoric times, as you walk past Urn Mount in Victoria Park. It will take you back to the days of wind-power, as you walk past the site of Wavertree Mill. It will recall the legends of long ago, as you stand by the Monks Well in Mill Lane. It will recall the 'pioneers' who built a new community, as you walk along Thingwall Road.

So, whether you are interested in the history of Wavertree, or simply curious about the Wavertree you see around you today ... read on.

THE PICTON CLOCK TO HILLS PLACE

The Picton Clock Tower - at the junction of Childwall Road, Church Road North and the High Street - has been a local landmark for over 100 years. It was presented to the people of Wavertree by Sir James Picton in 1884, having been designed by him as a memorial to his wife Sarah, who had died in 1879 after fifty years of happy marriage. Picton was a prominent local resident. Born in Liverpool, the son of a timber merchant, Picton became a well-known architect and surveyor. He moved to Wavertree in 1848, having designed and built himself a house - Sandy Knowe - in Mill Lane.

[Sir James Picton 1805-1889]

James Allanson Picton was a prominent member of both the Liverpool Town Council and the Wavertree Local Board of Health. In Liverpool he was Chairman of the Libraries Committee for almost forty years. As a mark of respect, one of the main library buildings was named after him in 1879, and two years later he was knighted by Queen Victoria in recognition of his 'high attainments and public services'. As well as being a linguist and seasoned traveller, Picton was a keen student of local history. His two-volume work entitled 'Memorials of Liverpool' remains one of the leading reference books on the city's buildings and personalities.

In order to begin the walk, you should cross - with great care - on to the central roundabout, and stand by the base of the clock tower. The inscription facing Church Road North reads 'Time wasted is existence; used is life'. It is difficult to think of a more fitting epitaph for Sir James Picton himself, who packed so much activity into his 83 years. Facing the High Street is another inscription, recording the dedication of the tower to 'his beloved wife Sarah Pooley'. After fifty years of marriage Sir James still seems to have referred to his wife by her maiden name! Before the days when everyone had watches or radio sets, the villagers of Wavertree would tell their children to 'go and see what the time is by Sarah Pooley'.

Sir James Picton deliberately chose this spot as the site for his gift, so that the clock could be seen by as many people as possible. It was the very centre of the old village. Before the Clock Tower was built it was the site of the 'Big Lamp', marking the parting of the ways for travellers to Old Swan, Childwall and Gateacre.

Stand with your back to the Picton Clock's timber doorway, facing towards Childwall Road and Mill Lane. Relatively few modern buildings are visible, and you can almost imagine yourself on the edge of the open countryside. The old Lock-up with its pointed roof stands on the Village Green, surrounded by trees. It was erected in 1796, principally as a place in which to accommodate drunks and other prisoners overnight. Wavertree was a very popular place in which to drink in those days - as it still is today! - and those who were unable to stagger home to Liverpool would be locked inside before being released or taken before a Magistrate the following morning.

Cross - again with great care - to the petrol station on the corner of the High Street and Church Road North. Walk a few yards down the High Street and stop on the corner of Waterloo Street, outside the Barley Mow pub. The building on the other corner - now the Modern Tandoori Restaurant with its entrance facing the High Street - is still recognisable as a Georgian house, its original doorway in Waterloo Street now blocked but retaining its pediment and pilasters. Between about 1850 and 1879 this building served as Wavertree's police station, and a small window survives inside from the old police cell.

Look across the High Street at the impressive brick facade of the Lamb Inn, with its archway leading to a yard and beer garden at the back. Often described as a 'Georgian coaching inn', the present building dates, in fact, from the 1850s. Although Baines's Lancashire Directory of 1825 lists the Lamb - together with the Coffee House and the Thatched House Tavern - it seems that the pub at that time was relatively small.

The brick archway of the present Lamb was not used for stage-coaches to pass through, but for William Dilworth's horse-drawn omnibuses which plied between Wavertree and the centre of Liverpool. Bus travel in those days was for the wealthy few. The single fare is said to have been 6d (6 old pence), which was well out of the reach of ordinary people.

In the days when many people were unable to read, pubs often took their name from an easily-recognisable symbol which could be displayed outside. Thus, in the early nineteenth century, township meetings in Wavertree were advertised as taking place 'at the Sign of the Lamb'. Nowadays there are other considerations, like brand image and corporate identity. In 1996 Allied Domecq, the owners of The Lamb, proposed to change its name to the Ferry & Firkin, following its transfer to their Firkin Brewery Co. subsidiary. Eventually - after protests by the Wavertree Society and others - the company agreed to allow the traditional name to remain on the front of the building. The new 'sub-title' is the Fold (as in sheep-fold) & Firkin: rather more relevant than the three-mile distant Ferry 'cross the Mersey!

Cross Waterloo Street and walk a few more paces down the High Street, stopping outside the bow-fronted shop (No.102) now called The Baluster. This kind of shop window must have been relatively common in Georgian Liverpool, but today this is the only surviving example. As a result this is a Grade II* ('two starred') Listed Building, along with the properties on either side which form part of the same block. The only other Wavertree buildings to be given such a high grading are the Blue Coat School and Chapel, and Holy Trinity Parish Church.

By 1980 the unique shop-front of No.102 - then occupied by Wavertree's last surviving traditional cobbler - was on the verge of disintegration. Fortunately, however, it was saved and expertly restored by the wood-turner who then began to sell his wares from the premises. It seems that this building has been the home of craftsmen for most of its days, for the 1846 Tithe Map shows it as a 'Sadlers Shop' occupied by John Gore, and Gore was still there in 1895. It was briefly occupied by Henry Broadbent, cycle manufacturer, about 1900, but by 1901 James Whittaker, boot dealer, had taken over.

Old photographs show that No.100 High Street - now 'High Street Antiques' - also had a small-paned shop window in the early part of the present century. It was, however, flat rather than bow-fronted. The 'Timberlines' shopfront at No.98 dates only from 1992, when the building became the head office of this local shopfitting and joinery company. It is in many ways a 'model' refurbishment of a front elevation, in stark contrast to some of the business premises lower down the High Street and in Picton Road.

Other shops used to exist on the opposite side of the High Street, but these were demolished many years ago. Earlier still, the Lamb had a bowling green and quoiting ground beyond the stable yard, but by 1900 both of these had been built on. The small houses just visible to the rear of the modern workshop premises are in Arnold Grove. One of them - No.12 - was in 1943 the birthplace of George Harrison, later to become world-famous as a member of the Beatles. Not surprisingly, in view of the fact that his family was rehoused in Speke when he was just 6 years old, George's memories of Wavertree are limited, but he has written: "It was OK that house ... Outside there was a little yard ... and for a period of time we had a little henhouse where we kept cockerels".

Walk just a few yards further on down the High Street, stopping when you reach a small side turning opposite the Cock & Bottle pub. This was formerly called 'Hills Place'. (The street nameplate survived until recently, high up on the side of the building you have just passed).

[Hills Place nameplate, removed 1996]

Until the 1930s Hills Place was the home of nine families, living in two blocks of small houses fronting on to a central yard. The houses were demolished as slums in about 1935, and the site - having since served as a school kitchen and as a joinery yard - is currently (June 1999) being converted into a pub car park.

HILLS PLACE TO WAVERTREE PLAYGROUND

From this side turning, look straight across the High Street at the Cock & Bottle pub. This view was once the subject of numerous picture postcards. Why? Because No.95 High Street, Wavertree - now the right-hand end of the pub - was known as the 'Smallest House in England'. Just 6 ft wide, and 14 ft from front to back, it was occupied as a house until 1925. There are stories of a husband and wife having raised eight

[Postcard view of No.95 High Street, circa 1900]

children in the house, and also of one very large resident who had to go upstairs sideways even after the staircase was widened to 16 inches from its original 8!

The facade of the 'Smallest House' was - at the suggestion of the Wavertree Society - renovated in 1998 by the owners, Bass Taverns, so as to more closely resemble its original appearance. The house itself was probably not all that old. The evidence of old maps suggests that it was built around 1850 in what had been a side passageway. (The Cock & Bottle was at that time a Temperance Coffee House). Much older is the building next door, now Done's betting shop. Building work in 1989 revealed an old sandstone lintel above the original front doorway, with the carved inscription 'J J L 1766'. These initials may, perhaps, have referred to John Leech, who is recorded as the licensee of The Lamb in 1777 and a trustee of Holy Trinity Church in 1793. Look above the modern shopfront - a replacement for one that was attached to the original house in Victorian times - and you will see some unusual geometric plasterwork below the eaves, together with a sash window which almost certainly retains its original 18th-century glass.

[The datestone uncovered in 1989 at No.97 High Street]

Still standing on the corner of Hills Place, look across the High Street towards the Town Hall. Wavertree Town Hall was built in 1872 as the headquarters of the Wavertree Local Board of Health. This was the body responsible for paving, lighting and cleaning the streets, providing sewers, and emptying middens in those parts of the Township where sewers had not been laid. It was formed in 1851 as the successor to the old Select Vestry, and comprised members elected by the ratepayers in the various districts of the Township.

The Town Hall was designed by a local architect: John Elliot Reeve, who lived in Sandown Lane. At the front were the offices of the Board, while at the back was a large ballroom together with the Board's stables and yard.

Wavertree was absorbed by the City of Liverpool in 1895 - along with the nearby Townships of West Derby and Walton - and the Town Hall served as a local rates collection and Registry Office for many years after the takeover. Then in 1979 - after a period of disuse which almost resulted in the building's demolition - the Town Hall was purchased by Mr Eric Rooke, a local businessman, who refurbished it as a public house, restaurant and functions suite and allowed the Wavertree Society to meet there on a regular basis.

Now walk down the High Street. As you pass the Town Hall, notice the decorative features of Reeve's typically Victorian design. Above the entrance is the Local Board's crest. The motto Sub Umbra Floresco means 'I flourish in the shade', almost certainly a reference to Wavertree's proud independence from neighbouring Liverpool.

[The crest on the front of the Town Hall]

The pair of small houses to the left of the Town Hall are a reminder of the original scale of the High Street. Originally it was a residential street - the heart of the old village - but gradually during the nineteenth century commercial uses took over. One such business - established in 1840 and discontinued as recently as

1984 - was Hicks' bakery. Hicks' old warehouse with its loading slot for sacks of flour - reminiscent of the early Liverpool dockland warehouses - can still be seen above No.83b High Street. William Hicks was born in Northamptonshire in about 1811 but - like so many others at that time - came north to find prosperity.

On reaching Prince Alfred Road, turn left out of the High Street. Cross the end of Pye Street, which is the side turning just beyond the petrol station. Across the road is Wavertree C. of E. Primary School. This was originally built in 1867 as a so-called 'National' school, the founding body being the National Society for the Education of the Poor according to the Principles of the Church of England. This was before the days of State education for all. The architect was Edward A. Heffer, whose use of coloured brickwork is typical of the period.

Having walked past the school and its new playground, cross Prince Alfred Road and go through the gap in the railings opposite No.33, on to the green expanse known as 'The Mystery'. Turn round and you will see an interesting variety of old houses fronting on to Prince Alfred Road, many of them - such as the cream painted block of private flats, once a row of five houses known as Hope Terrace - having unobstructed views over the park.

The present-day Wavertree Playground - better known as the Mystery (or 'Mizzy' for short) ever since it opened to the public in 1895 - was once the grounds of a large house known as The Grange, which stood alongside Prince Alfred Road just 100 yards or so from this point. From 1852 onwards this was the residence of a wealthy Liverpool merchant, the Irish-born Samuel R. Graves. When Graves moved from Falkner Square to Wavertree - and when he became Liverpool's Member of Parliament in 1865 - Prince Alfred Road was called 'Cow Lane', a reminder of its origins as one of the old farm tracks leading out of the village. Not exactly a prestige address for one of Liverpool's leading citizens! Graves must have been very pleased when, in 1866, he played host to Queen Victoria's second son - Prince Alfred, Duke of Edinburgh - and the Local Board agreed to rename Cow Lane in honour of the prince's stay. (Older Wavertree residents remember the time when the C. of E. School was nicknamed 'Cow Lane College'). Prince Alfred was visiting Liverpool to lay the foundation stone of the Myrtle Street Children's Infirmary and to open a new dock entrance ('Alfred Dock') on the other side of the River Mersey.

Samuel Graves died suddenly of a heart attack in the Euston Hotel, London, in 1873, aged 54. He was obviously a much-respected MP, for on the day of his funeral all business ceased in the centre of Liverpool for two hours, and the funeral itself, at the Toxteth Park Cemetery in Smithdown Road, is said to have attracted a crowd of 50,000 mourners. There is a statue of him inside St George's Hall.

[The Grange, demolished 1895]

WAVERTREE PLAYGROUND TO ROSE COTTAGE

In 1895 the Grange was demolished, and it was assumed that - like other mansions around the village - its grounds would be bought by house-builders. During the previous 25 years almost the whole of the area between Smithdown Road and Picton Road had become covered with tightly-packed housing: decent enough, its spacing dictated by the building bye-laws, but with virtually no provision for open space.

The Liverpool Daily Post conjured up a picture of the area round Wellington Road - the area downhill from Wavertree Playground - as it was in 1895:

"Wavertree ... is, as it were, one of the arms which, like other great towns, Liverpool, in the manner of a vast octopus of bricks and mortar, stretches into the country along the main roads which lead into it. At the point where this area of Wavertree joins on to the body of the city we have the brick and mortar plague now passing through its acutest stage ... streets of cottages awkwardly fitted in anywhere, or leading into other streets, which seem in turn to lead nowhere. There are villainous-looking wastes, whose surfaces present an alternation of stagnant pools and hillocks of tipped rubbish, a lonely public-house or two built as speculations in 'futures' on what may turn out to be 'desirable corner lots', a grimy brick church, and board schools ... but ... the wastes are slowly and by degrees disappearing before the enterprise of the inevitable builder".

Then suddenly, in May 1895, it was announced that an anonymous donor had purchased the Grange estate together with some adjoining properties, and was presenting the whole 108 acres to the City of Liverpool. The donor had levelled and grassed the area - eradicating the ornamental lake that was once a feature of the grounds - and suggested the name 'Wavertree Playground'. It was to be a venue for organised sports, and a place for children to run about in, not a park for 'promenading' in the Victorian tradition. He expressed the hope that the City Council "might approve of giving it a fair trial for this purpose ... before appropriating it for any other use".

[Certificate presented at the opening of Wavertree Playground]

The mysterious donor's offer was accepted by the Council; the Playground was opened by the Lord Mayor amid great rejoicing on 7th September 1895. There was a march past of 12,000 children, after which, the Daily Post reported, "the children were liberally regaled with cakes and milk". Juvenile sports, a gymnastics exhibition and Morris Dancing followed, and finally "for upwards of two hours, the sky was brilliant" with a fireworks display watched by an estimated 60,000 people.

The new park was immediately nicknamed 'The Mystery'. At the time the Press speculated that the donor might be Philip Holt - a shipowner who himself lived on the edge of Sefton Park - but this was neither confirmed nor denied. Looking across the park (and the newly-built Athletics Centre) towards the city centre skyline, the foresight of preserving such a 'green lung' can be appreciated today just as it was in 1895. If Holt was indeed the Mystery man, Wavertree has a lot to thank him for.

Now walk down alongside the school's playground fence, turning right to reach the old sandstone boundary wall which now separates the park from the Prince Alfred Nursing Home. Follow this wall round as far as the electricity sub-station, then leave the Mystery through the gate to your right. You are now standing alongside Wavertree Gardens, one of the few surviving examples of Sir Lancelot Keay's tenement blocks. Built in 1935, the 72 flats were designed to house families displaced by local slum clearance in Pye Street, Hills Place and other similar 'courts' off the High Street.

Lancelot Keay was Liverpool's Director of Housing from 1925 onwards, and also City Architect from 1939 until his retirement in 1948. He initially specialised in producing very attractive, low density suburban estates, but during the 1930s the scale of the rehousing problem, together with a new system of government grants, encouraged him to increase densities. Keay designed a number of tenement blocks - all euphemistically named 'Gardens' - some of them, like this one, neo-Georgian but most of them in a modernistic style inspired by Continental architects. In 1935 Wavertree Gardens was visited and admired by delegates to the 14th International Housing and Town Planning Congress. Now, however, the block is sadly neglected, and its future is uncertain.

[The exit from the old tram-sheds]

Before entering the High Street, look down beneath your feet. You should be able to make out different types of stone: sandstone blocks on the outside and smaller granite setts in the centre of the path. This is a - probably unique - reminder of the days of horse-drawn trams in Liverpool. Wavertree Gardens was built partly on the site of the Liverpool Tramways Company's depot and stables, and the granite setts were laid between the tram tracks so as to avoid the road surface being eroded by the constant clatter of horseshoes. This is a feature which could so easily be lost during the course of 'improvements' to the footpath.

On reaching the High Street, turn right and walk to the light-controlled pedestrian crossing. The setting-back of the flats at this point marks the City Engineer's 'improvement line' which was defined - long before

Conservation Areas were first thought of - on the assumption that virtually all of the High Street's old buildings would eventually disappear. Cross the road when it is safe to do so.

The building on the far side of the crossing - now a bar called 'Cuffs' - is still recognisably a police station, though it has not been used for that purpose since 1967. If you look upwards, to the left, you will see the Lancashire County coat of arms carved in sandstone, and the intertwined date '1879' nearby. Gargoyles project from the eaves.

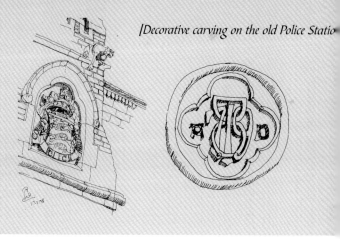

[Decorative carving on the old Police Statio

Walk down the High Street past the Rose Vaults pub. On the 1846 Tithe Map this small building is described as a 'house, beer house and malt kiln' occupied by John Anderton. Anderton also owned the Rose Brewery (on the corner of Picton Road and Wellington Road) and residential property including Anderton Square (a 'court' on the site of Wavertree Gardens).

More roses are to be found (nominally) just beyond the pub: a landscaped area once the site of a row of small cottages. For many years, following the demolition of the cottages by the City Council, this area lay totally derelict and overgrown. In 1979, however, the Wavertree Society had the idea of transforming it into a Rose Garden. The Society's scheme was a prizewinner in the Merseyside Improved Neighbourhood Competition - organised by Merseyside Improved Houses to celebrate their 50 years as a housing association - and as a result the idea became a reality.

The name Rose Garden was suggested by the site's location, sandwiched between the Rose Vaults and Rose Cottage (No.35 High Street). Continue walking until you reach the front gate of Rose Cottage, with its unusual cylindrical sandstone gate-piers. Rose Cottage was once one of the showpieces of Wavertree, with its picturesque garden hidden behind the carefully-shaped privet hedge. Sadly, in 1986 it fell into dereliction and the garden was totally destroyed. Fortunately, Rose Cottage is now occupied and the garden and hedge are once again being taken care of.

Rose Cottage has been described as a last vestige of rural Wavertree. It is probably not the oldest building in the village - 1800 has been suggested as a possible date - but its roof of 'tun' (large) slates is noteworthy and its long front garden is a unique survival on this side of the High Street, where so many of the old houses have been converted to shops.

[Rose Cottage]

ROSE COTTAGE TO ORFORD STREET

Look across to the other (south) side of the High Street. To the right of Wavertree Gardens is a row of three Georgian houses faced in stucco over sandstone. Further to the right is a row of six brick houses, originally known as 'Grove Terrace'. Like Rose Cottage, all of these houses are now Listed Buildings and alterations to their external appearance are discouraged.

In the early nineteenth century, when these houses were built, Wavertree was changing from a sleepy agricultural village to a fairly exclusive dormitory area for Liverpool. These were 'town houses' - in the style which was fashionable in Liverpool itself (Hope Street, Canning Street, etc.) - but with the advantage of views over open countryside.

Continue walking down the High Street until you reach the Wavertree Car Centre sales site. Just opposite is Wavertree's newest Listed Building: the telephone box outside No.24. This is an example of the 'K6' type Jubilee Kiosk - designed in 1935 by Sir Giles Gilbert Scott, the architect of Liverpool's Anglican Cathedral - which, although once very common, is now being phased out. This particular box became a Listed Building in 1989, having been selected for preservation because of its position within the Wavertree Village Conservation Area.

The occupier of No.24 High Street in the 1860s was William Quiggin, a Liverpool shipbuilder best remembered for the blockade runners which his firm supplied to the Confederate cause in the American Civil War. Quiggin, who had moved here from Mill Street in Toxteth, also engaged in property development in Wavertree, being responsible for building what became the Prince Alfred pub and nearby shops.

Next door, at No.22, the 1861 Census records Dr Edward Swinden, a general practitioner and surgeon born in Yorkshire. He lived there with his wife, born in Staffordshire, their five children and three servants. At No.26 - the slightly smaller house to the left - was the Hampshire-born merchant Richard Phillips, his Denbighshire-born wife, three children and a single servant.

The passageway alongside No.22 - separating Grove Terrace from the Post Office - is still officially called Paradise Gardens: formerly the address of a cluster of tiny cottages on the edge of The Mystery which, to the dismay of the residents, were demolished as 'slums' in the 1960s. The red-brick block which includes the Post Office (as well as 'Chequers' pub) was built in 1888 by the Bank of Liverpool, to house its Wavertree branch.

The used-car sales area, by which you are currently standing, occupies the site of Nos 17-21 High Street, a block of three houses which were set back behind a tall brick wall. In the late nineteenth century this was a place of pilgrimage for American tourists just as Arnold Grove - George Harrison's birthplace - is today. For between 1828 and 1831 Mrs Felicia Dorothea Hemans lived at No.17 High Street, and Mrs Hemans was one of the best-known poetesses of her age. Famous in America as the author of 'The Landing of the Pilgrim Fathers', which is traditionally recited on Thanksgiving Day, she is remembered in Britain for just one line: 'The boy stood on the burning deck ...' (from her poem 'Casabianca'). Born in Duke Street, Liverpool, in 1793, Mrs Hemans moved from Abergele in North Wales to Wavertree at the height of her fame, but moved away to Dublin after only three years. Reputedly she left

[Mrs Felicia Hemans 1793-1835]

Wavertree because the natives were too inquisitive!

At No.19 - the middle house of the long-demolished block - lived Dr James Kenyon in the 1840s. Born near Lancaster in 1814, he was another example of a professional man who moved to Liverpool and then chose to settle in Wavertree. It was Dr Kenyon who bought the field behind his house and created Orford Street, which he named after his wife's family. Later on, the house was the residence of Mr Patrick O'Connor, an Irish-born ironmonger, of whom more later.

Before continuing along the High Street, look at the gable-end wall of No.15, which is the building immediately adjacent to the car-sales area. This was obviously at one time a house with a front garden, but at some time during the nineteenth century the garden disappeared under a new shop-front. For many years, from 1851 onwards, the shop was occupied by Frederick Newcombe, linen draper.

Continue walking along the High Street, and stop on the next corner (Sandown Lane). Looking across the main road, you can see the 'join' between Wavertree High Street and Picton Road. Picton Road was originally called Wavertree Lane, then became Wavertree Road, but in 1883 the Local Board resolved to rename it in honour of their retiring Chairman, Sir James Picton, who was about to present the Township with the Clock Tower.

Now look at the tall brick building - No.203 Picton Road, currently occupied by a TV rental firm - on the corner of Sandown Lane. Clearly this was at one time a warehouse: the sack loading slot is still there. Look more closely at the blind first-floor window, on the corner, and you may just be able to decipher two faded inscriptions behind the burglar-alarm box. One - in gold lettering - reads 'Francis and McKay', the bakers and confectioners, who occupied the building until the 1960s . Much

[The inscription on 203 Picton Road]

older, however, is the one in brown capitals: 'Flour & Provender Dealer'. This is a reminder of the original occupier of the building: Charles Taylor, the very last tenant of Wavertree Mill.

Wavertree Mill - one of the most ancient windmills recorded in the Liverpool area - stood near Woolton

Road (see Sections 10 and 11 of this walk) and operated until 1889. With the mill site having been redeveloped in 1986, this old flour warehouse is one of the last surviving relics of Charles Taylor's famous local enterprise. It is probably too much to hope that the faded inscription - in many ways a miraculous survival from the past - will remain visible for many years to come.

Before starting to walk along Sandown Lane, look towards and beyond the pedestrian traffic-lights in Picton Road. This 'rural' stretch of Picton Road was all that separated Wavertree Village from the rest of Liverpool in 1895, when the city's boundaries were extended, but it was not long before the gap had been filled. The new buildings included three which were the work of the Corporation Surveyor, Thomas Shelmerdine: the Technical Institute (1898) on the corner of Pearson Street, the Library (1902) and the Public Baths (1904). By this means the City Council literally cemented its links with the newly-absorbed Township of Wavertree.

[Photograph of Sandown Lane, circa 1890, by Edward Newton Ellis]

Now walk along Sandown Lane. Stop on the corner of Orford Street, in front of the Edinburgh pub. Every house in Orford Street is a Listed Building, and undoubtedly it is the most attractive street in Wavertree Village. The houses are all of a similar style, though they differ considerably in detail, suggesting that several builders were involved. Contemporary maps and Census records reveal that almost all of the houses were built between 1848 and 1852. By the time of the 1851 Census 24 of the houses - out of the present day total of 36 - were occupied, the residents including 6 'annuitants', 2 joiners, a plasterer, an upholsterer, a gardener, a cart owner, a 'professor of dancing', a school master, a printer, a master mariner and a banker's accountant. In 1875 Gore's Directory listed the occupations of 32 of the householders, including 5 gardeners, 4 coachmen, 3 joiners, 2 blacksmiths and 2 artists. So, by and large, the residents of Orford Street earned their living not by commuting to Liverpool, but by 'serving' the wealthy inhabitants of the larger houses elsewhere in the village.

As already mentioned, the laying-out of Orford Street was the idea of Dr Kenyon, whose High Street residence backed on to it and whose wife was Ann Orford (daughter of a wealthy merchant, William Orford of Everton). This pattern - of professional or business men acting as local property developers - seems to have been quite common in Victorian Wavertree.

ORFORD STREET TO SANDOWN PARK

The name of the Edinburgh pub is another reminder of Prince Alfred's visit to Wavertree. The houses on the opposite side of Sandown Lane seem from the evidence of maps to be amongst the oldest in the area. The present numbers 3, 5 and 7 are shown on Leather's map of 1836. No.17 (originally, it appears, No.11) is a double fronted house which was the home of John Elliot Reeve, the architect of Wavertree Town Hall.

Next door to No.17 is 'Alma Terrace', a row of four houses - two pairs of semis linked together - which we know from local records to have been built by Mr William Pearson, a prominent local builder, in 1855. That was a year after the Battle of the Alma, an Allied victory during the Crimean war; hence the name.

It has been said that - in terms of house types - Wavertree is a microcosm of Liverpool. Certainly there can be few streets as varied as Sandown Lane, which has examples from almost every period from the 1830s to the 1980s. A deed dated 1803 mentions "a lane proposed to be called Sandown Lane" leading out of the High Street, but it was a long time before the development of the street began to gather momentum. One of the most startling arrivals must have been 'Sandown Terrace', the row of 12 large terraced houses on the right-hand side of the street. Stand opposite the former Wesleyan Methodist chapel (built in 1837) just beyond Wesley Place, and look up at the red-and-gold painted pediment in the centre of the Terrace.

[The Sandown Terrace pediment]

Sandown Terrace is shown on the Wavertree Tithe Map of 1846, but not on Leather's map of 1836. On the Tithe Map the buildings are described as 'cottages': possibly to avoid the payment of window tax. They were owned by William Bennett, an ironfounder with business premises in Whitechapel, Liverpool. His origins were in Chester, which must account for the three wheatsheaves - symbols of the County of Cheshire - in the pediment design. Bennett was later to become Mayor of Liverpool, but in 1846 he was still a young man. Why he decided to build such an impressive terrace of houses in a rural backwater like Sandown Lane is not at all clear!

The iron railings in front of Sandown Terrace date from the early 1980s, when the residents formed an Association to restore the facade to its original, uniform appearance with the help of Inner City grants. Until that happened, the houses presented a mixture of different coloured paintwork and pebbledash, and windows in a variety of styles.

The occupants of Sandown Terrace at the time of the 1851 Census included a butcher, a cotton broker, a customs officer, a retired grocer, a nurseryman, a ship broker, a 'gentlewoman teacher' and a tobacco manufacturer, along with two clerks and two 'house proprietors'. Only one of the householders had been born in Wavertree, and 4 in Liverpool; the birthplaces of the others included Scotland, Yorkshire, Devon, Ireland and the Isle of Man. Each of the households employed a 'living in' servant, apart from one which had two servants. Like the householders, the servants had been drawn from far afield: 5 of them had been born in Liverpool, but 3 were from Wales, 2 from Ireland, and one had been born in the West Indies.

Now continue along Sandown Lane. The first turning on the right is North Drive. Don't turn into North Drive just yet; it will be covered later on in the walk. Instead, cross to the other side of Sandown Lane and turn into Northdale Road. The houses here are of the standard 'bye-law' design which Liverpool house-builders built by the thousand between 1875 and 1914. Using good quality but monotonous materials imported by the trainload from the brickworks and slate quarries of North Wales, small local building firms - themselves dominated by the Welsh - covered all the open land they could find with serried ranks of solidly-built houses for the artisan and the clerk. In this case the builders were Messrs Jones & Hughes: John Jones (called 'John Jones Drinkwater' owing to his refusal to give bricklayers the customary 'price of a pint' on completing the first house in a block!) and John Hughes, both of whom came from Anglesey. The predominance of railwaymen among the early residents gave this locality its one-time nickname: 'the Railway Parish'.

Walk along Northdale Road to the first cross-roads, then turn right into Eastdale Road. Twenty yards along, turn down the side-entry alongside the first terrace of houses you come to (behind the houses you have just passed in Northdale Road). Then turn left in front of the 'surprise' pair of cottage gardens.

This is one of the best-hidden corners of old Wavertree. The road which serves these semi-detached houses, together with the row of fifteen houses beyond, is called Salisbury Terrace:

named, no doubt, after the Marquess of Salisbury, one-time Lord of the Manor. All of the houses are shown on the Wavertree Tithe Map of 1846, though not on Leather's map of 1836.

Until about 1910, the residents of Salisbury Terrace had unobstructed views across the grounds of a large mansion: 'Westdale House', which stood near the present junction of Rathbone Road with Sunningdale Road and had a driveway leading down to a lodge on Picton Road. Westdale House had been the home of Mr John Stock - a leading Liverpool cotton broker - but after 1910 its only relic was the name Westdale Road and all the other 'dales' nearby. This was before the days of town planning controls, and the fact that the new houses in Eastdale Road presented their backsides to the older houses in Salisbury Terrace was obviously felt to be of no consequence. A more striking example of rigid adherence to the building bye-laws - and the desire of the builders to cram as many houses as possible on to the space available - is difficult to imagine.

In 1851 Salisbury Terrace was home to a wide variety of individuals. Of the 15 heads of household recorded by the Census, 7 were retired (including one man described as a 'Chelsea Pentioner'); the others comprising 4 clerks, a bookkeeper, a chronometer maker, a linen draper and a dress maker. It will be no surprise to learn that none of them had been born in Wavertree, and only 3 were from Liverpool; the birthplaces of the rest including Derbyshire, Essex, Scotland, Ireland and Flanders!

Although similar in size to the houses of Orford Street, the houses in Salisbury Terrace have back gardens up to 75 feet in length, behind which are similar-sized gardens belonging to the much larger houses in

Sandown Lane. The Tithe Map of 1846 lists the owners of Nos 1-9 as the Sandown Building Society: one of the few references to such an organisation in Wavertree at that time.

Walk along the 'back entry' of Eastdale Road, which is a few feet higher than the carriageway of Salisbury Terrace. Cross the end of Sunningdale Road, and turn right - into Long Lane - when you reach the T-junction at the far end. Then walk along to the crossroads.

Long Lane is one of the oldest roads in Wavertree - it appears on some early maps as a continuation of the meandering Pighue (or Picko) Lane - yet the part of it immediately east of this point is still unadopted by the City Council. Before crossing to the other side of Sandown Lane, walk to the pillar-box which, you will soon discover, lacks any sort of royal cipher. This box was installed here as long ago as 1865: the date and the maker's name - Cochrane Grove & Co of Dudley - are cast in metal near the base. It is one of the few surviving examples of the so-called First National Standard type of box, a design that was introduced in 1859 but quickly superseded owing to the fact that rainwater could so easily enter the slot. In 1982, when it was temporarily removed for refurbishment, the Post Office revealed that only three others of its type remained in use.

[The pillar box in Sandown

Why should a pillar-box have been erected in this particular location? Look across Long Lane for a clue: a single-storey house in Sandown Road with a carved sandstone pillar alongside. The stone pillar was one of a pair which, in the nineteenth century, supported gates facing across to the end of Sandown Lane, while the house was the gatekeeper's lodge. This was the entrance to Sandown Park, an exclusive residential estate laid out in the late 1840s by local architect Cornelius Sherlock. As in the case of similar estates elsewhere on Merseyside - such as Grassendale Park and Rock Park - plots were made available for the building of large villas (either detached or semi-detached) whose residents could enjoy the tranquillity and prestige of landscaped grounds without the expense of maintaining the whole estate themselves. By the 1860s about twenty houses had been built in the Park - the householders listed in Gore's Directory for 1862 including 9 merchants, 3 brokers, 2 attorneys, a brassfounder and a silversmith - and it was obviously felt that a local pillar-box was fully justified.

SANDOWN PARK TO ST MARY'S CHURCH

Now cross over to the 'private road' portion of Long Lane, by the electricity sub-station, and walk along about 50 yards. Looking across the playing-fields to your left, you should be able to see in the distance a pale-coloured mansion. This is Sandown Hall, one-time home of the Hornby family and, more recently, Crawfords Biscuits' social club.

[Sandown Hall circa 1830, from a drawing by James Brierley]

In 1821 Sandown Hall was advertised for sale: "The Mansion, Stables, Outbuildings, Grounds comprising the Eastern part of the beautiful and valuable estate in Wavertree called Sandown. 19 Statute acres formerly in occupation of Mr Willis Earle". It seems likely that Sandown Hall had been built for this Mr Earle, a coal merchant with a yard in Stanhope Street, Liverpool, in about 1810. The next recorded occupier of Sandown Hall was George Littledale, from Whitehaven, who married in 1822 but died, aged 43, only four years later.

About 1827 the most famous family ever to occupy Sandown Hall - and indeed any of the mansions around Wavertree Village - moved in. These were the Hornbys: Hugh Hornby, a merchant specialising in trade with Russia, and his wife Louise Cortazzi, daughter of a former British Consul in Smyrna. Hugh Hornby - whose roots were in Kirkham, near Blackpool - had travelled extensively before settling down in Everton in 1823. Everton was at that time a much sought-after place to live - "for the salubrity of its air, and its vicinity to the sea, it may not inaptly be called the Montpelier of the county", commented Baines's Lancashire Directory in 1824 - and Hugh and his brother Joseph Hornby were just two of the many wealthy men who had made it their home. (The family firm - H.& J. Hornby & Co. - had its offices in the Exchange Buildings, behind Liverpool Town Hall).

By 1826 Hugh had decided to leave Everton for the even more rural surroundings of Wavertree, where the Sandown estate on the slopes of Olive Mount offered similar benefits of an elevated situation, fresh breezes and views of the setting sun. In 1851 Hugh and Louise still had five children (aged 13-25) living at home, and the Census records them as employing ten resident servants at Sandown Hall: a governess, a butcher, a coachman, a groom, a cook, a lady's maid, a laundry maid, a house maid, an 'under house maid' and a dairy maid.

The Hornby family was well-known in Liverpool for a number of different reasons. Hugh Hornby was Mayor of the town in 1838, having been a member of the Council for many years. His nephew Thomas Dyson Hornby was a merchant, and Chairman of the Mersey Docks & Harbour Board: Hornby Dock having been named after him in 1884. Most celebrated of all, though, was to be Hugh's eldest son, Hugh Frederick

Hornby ('Fred' to his friends) who took little interest in business affairs but spent a lifetime amassing a collection of rare books, prints and autographs in his house - Sandown Lodge - which was situated only a short distance away from the Hall. When H. F. Hornby died in 1899 he bequeathed this collection to the City, together with the sum of £10,000 to pay for a building to house it in. The result today is the Hornby Library, part of the Central Libraries complex in William Brown Street.

One Hornby not connected in any way with Sandown Hall was Frank Hornby, the inventor of Meccano and manufacturer of Hornby trains. Although these products were made within half a mile of here - in Binns Road, just within the old Wavertree Township boundary - there was no family connection whatsoever with the 'merchant' Hornbys.

[Ordnance Survey map of the Sandown Lane area, circa 1849]

Sandown Hall provides a good, if saddening, example of the way in which Wavertree's rural character has gradually been eroded. Already by 1821 the western part of the estate had been sold off, and in the late 1840s it became the site of Sandown Park. Then in the 1920s - following the death of the three Hornby sisters who had inherited the estate from their widowed mother - Sandown Hall was acquired by Crawfords Biscuits (whose factory was close to Meccano in Binns Road) for use as a sports and social club. Sports pitches were laid out, and a few houses for senior staff were built in the grounds. With the declining interest in outdoor recreation, some of the pitches later fell into disuse, and in 1977 a large part of the estate was sold to Merseyside Improved Houses. Meanwhile, a new estate of private homes had been built on the other side of Long Lane, on the Wavertree Recreation Company's tennis courts.

In 1989 the City Council announced its intention of selling-off its own part of the Sandown estate: the playing-fields across which you are currently looking. Fortunately a campaign of resistance - led by the Wavertree Society - was successful on this occasion, and the field is now designated as Public Open Space. A few months later, however, planning permission was granted for the building of yet more houses on what remained of the company sports ground, behind the Hall.

At the time of writing (June 1999) the future of Sandown Hall is uncertain. It has been privately owned since 1990, but plans for its re-use have come to nothing and, in recent years, the condition of the building has deteriorated dramatically. In December 1996, following a Public Inquiry, the Secretary of State for the Environment rejected the owners' application to demolish the Hall (a Listed Building since 1952). The Secretary of State agreed with the Planning Inspector's comment that "to allow demolition ... could ... raise doubts about the principles of preservation. It could suggest acquiescence with owners who, for whatever reasons, have allowed a building to fall into such a dilapidated state".

Now turn round and walk back to Sandown Lane. On your left - out of sight behind the high wall - is

Wavertree's Cricket Ground, established in the nineteenth century by a private company. In 1892 "the danger occasioned to persons passing through Long Lane by reason of cricket balls" and "the nuisance produced by the deposit in the lane of mown grass from the cricket field" were being complained of to the Local Board of Health by certain wealthy residents of Sandown Park, but fortunately the club and the ground have both survived intact to the present day.

Walk down Sandown Lane alongside the cricket ground wall. On your right are the large town-houses which back on to Salisbury Terrace. Architecturally they are an interesting mixture, having been the work of numerous different builders between about 1840 and 1910. The only ones to be Listed are Nos. 35, 37, 47 and 49, which were among the first to be built. In 1851 No. 37 was the home of 28-year-old Charles Byford - an auctioneer born in Suffolk - his Liverpool-born wife and Yorkshire-born servant. Next door at No.35 lived Thomas Thompson (also 28) an 'East India merchant's managing clerk' born in Liverpool, his wife and baby daughter, and two servants - perhaps sisters - from Flint.

Continue as far as North Drive (the first road on the left). On the left-hand corner is one of the most unusual buildings in Sandown Lane, a pair of stuccoed semi-detached houses with Gothic archways and other details, including tiny heads carved in stone. The roof is of particular interest, being clad in purple and grey bands of 'fish scale' shaped slates. These houses - now numbered 1 and 3 North Drive, Victoria Park - were

*[Decorat
feature on N
North Dri*

built in about 1840. They are shown on the Tithe Map of 1846, together with two large detached villas opposite and one further along North Drive. In fact this was the start of a speculative estate called 'Olive Park', but the original scheme does not seem to have got very far.

It was the 1860s before Olive Park became Victoria Park and house-building began in earnest. The minute books of the Wavertree Local Board of Health record a steady stream of plans being submitted for approval from 1862 onwards, when Mr William Webb's plan for the roads which became North and South Drives was given the go-ahead. As with Sandown Park, the idea was that individuals could purchase building plots on which to erect either detached or semi-detached dwellings of suitably grand dimensions. There were to be plenty of trees, but no lodges and no gates.

The residents of Victoria Park were drawn from a slightly 'lower rung' on the social ladder than those in Sandown Park. They were not the brokers, the 'merchant princes' and the shipowners, but instead a range of business and professional men, many of them earning their living locally within the village rather than in

VICTORIA PARK, WAVERTREE—W

Sandown lane

Harper Rev. Stephen "The Manse"
3 Pennant Carl gentleman "Bremon Lodge"
5 Victoria Park School "Foveron"
Misses Gudgen and Godfrey
7 Badnall William W. wine merchant
9 Brown Valentine Somers, Esq. barrister-at-law
9 Browne, The Misses "Ingledene"
11 Robinson Thomas gentleman "Beech Leigh"
17 Comer Miss Evelyn Mary "Mayfield"
19 Rockliff Mrs. Mary H. "Lauriston"
Rockliff Robert A. stationer
Rockliff George solicitor "Lauriston"
21 Horrock's John corn & flour dealer "Winniesville"
23 Brodbelt Miss Emily "Bleak House"
Orme Jas. confctnr. "Laburnum Villa"
Smith Mrs. Annie "Urn Mount"
Cunningham Mrs. Frances Mary "Urn Mount"
Bristow Wm. gentleman "Rock Hey"
Archer Walter J. manufacturing optician "Tytherley"
Archer Frederick W. manufacturing optician "Tytherley"
Neal Thomas gentleman "Holmfield"
Comerford Mrs. Mary P. "Laragh"
Blyth John corn mcht. "The Hollies"
2 Roberts Miss Margaret D. —— "Laurel Bank"
4 Taplin Benjamin E. artist

Liverpool. Gore's Directory for 1898 lists thirty different occupations here, ranging from an Artist to an Umbrella Manufacturer. A walk through Victoria Park gives you a good idea of the varying architectural tastes of the middle classes in Victorian Wavertree.

Walk along North Drive, and stop opposite the present-day parish church of St Mary. Impressive buildings like this, complete with masonry spire, were a feature of the enclosed residential estates of this period; no doubt the promoters took special steps to encourage them as a sort of status symbol amid the greenery. In fact the original St Mary's Church was in Sandown Park - on a site later occupied by Mabel Fletcher College - but it was destroyed by bombing during the Second World War. This church in Victoria Park belonged to the Wesleyan Methodists, who built it in 1872 to replace their much smaller chapel in Sandown Lane.

ST MARY'S CHURCH TO THE MONKS WELL

Having passed the church, look along South Drive which branches off to the right at this point. On the left, set back behind some trees, is the present St Mary's Rectory, converted from an old coach house and stables in 1982. These buildings were another common feature of such Victorian estates, for many of the residents employed coachmen and grooms as well as indoor servants. Nos 10 and 12 North Drive - the semi-detached pair alongside the outbuildings - are typical of the early housing built in Victoria Park. Cross the road to the corner of South Drive and you will see the date 1865 ornately displayed above the front door of No.10.

[The doorway of No.10 North Drive]

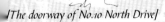

Continue walking along North Drive. There has been some infilling of modern semis, but most of the houses date from the late 1860s. Some of them have been subdivided into flats, though nowadays there is an encouraging trend towards single-family occupation when properties change hands. Just past No.16a on the right-hand side, you will notice a very large side garden, with large rocks punctuating its uneven surface. Older residents of Wavertree remember 'Scotch Betty', an eccentric lady fond of chasing small boys out of her garden! The bumps are said to mark her dogs' graves.

Cross the road at this point and stand by the gate of No.27. Looking up at the gable-end wall of No.29, you will notice a painted terracotta urn set into the brickwork. This commemorates an intriguing discovery made when the house was being built in 1867, which put Wavertree firmly on the map of Prehistoric Merseyside. For while the foundations for this pair of semi-detached houses were being dug, the workmen uncovered a number of Bronze Age burial urns - dating from before 1000 BC - containing human remains and flint arrowheads. Several urns were smashed by over-eager treasure hunters, but two were recovered and presented to the Liverpool Museum, where they remain - as the 'Wavertree Urns' - to this day.

[The Wavertree Urns]

Walk past No.29 ('Urn House') to the adjoining No.31 ('Urn Mount') which has another terracotta urn set into the gable-end wall. Back in 1867 the two houses were being built for Patrick O'Connor, the High Street ironmonger.

Continuing along North Drive, the next four houses on the left - together with the large pair of semis opposite - are all Listed Buildings. After the Cross & Passion Convent (formerly a house called Rock Hey) comes No.35 North Drive, a fine example of a detached villa residence of the 1860s. Until stone-cleaning work obliterated the inscription, the gate-piers of this house used to bear the name 'Tytherley': Mr Richard Phillips - who had this house built for himself in 1864 - having been born in East Tytherley, Hampshire. The 1851 Census had described Phillips - then living in the High Street - as a 'Book Keeper', but by 1871 he was a 'Manager for United States Merchant and landowner' living here in Victoria Park with his wife, four grown-up children and two domestic servants (housemaid and cook).

[Gate pier of No.35 North Drive, photographed in 1983]

Clearly, as Wavertree Village became busier and its inhabitants more prosperous, a green oasis like Victoria Park was a very attractive alternative to the High Street only 300 yards away. It also, however, drew its early residents from much further afield. Next door to Phillips - at the present No.37 North Drive, then called 'Holmfield' -

the 1871 Census records Mr Allan Hanckel, a 40-year-old merchant born in South Carolina. He lived there with his 25-year-old wife (born in West Derby), three young children and six servants, including a housemaid from Wolverhampton and a 'trained sick nurse' from Scotland.

Now continue along North Drive until you are outside No.49, opposite the end of South Drive. By 1893 - when the first large-scale Ordnance Survey map of the area was produced - a total of 60 houses had been built in Victoria Park (12 detached and 48 semi-detached) suggesting that it was much more of a commercial success than its near neighbour Sandown Park.

The title deeds of properties in Victoria Park refer to the area as the Lake House Estate. Lake House itself - or 'Monkswell House' as it was later known - was demolished long ago, but the tall, buttressed wall of its garden can still be seen on the left-hand side of South Drive.

Keep on walking along North Drive, then cross the road after passing the end of Monkswell Drive. The name of this typical cul-de-sac of 1930s semis is a further reminder of Monkswell House which formerly stood on the site. Turn the corner from North Drive into Mill Lane and you will see the sandstone cross from which the old house got its name: the 'Monks Well' itself.

Baines's Lancashire Directory of 1825 says of Wavertree: "Here is a well at which charitable contributions were anciently collected, bearing the following monkish inscription in antique letters -
  Qui non dat quod Habet
  Doemon Infra Ridet. Anno 1414.

Which may be thus freely translated: -
  He who here does nought bestow
  The Devil laughs at him below".
Moss's Liverpool Guide of 1796 had gone further, suggesting that "an old monastic looking house" alongside had been "inhabited by some religious order, who might thus request alms towards their support".

The well is undoubtedly ancient. It used to stand further back from the road, at a point where pure water bubbled out from the sandstone of Olive Mount. In the masonry beneath the original cross was an archway, under which a few steps gave access to the stone cistern or chamber containing the water. The Wavertree Enclosure Act of 1768 referred to "the through tunnel, channel or stone gutter, lately laid and made ... to carry and convey water from the said well or basin into another ... lately also made, erected and built, in the highway or road adjoining". Apparently the owner of Lake House had objected to the villagers walking over his lawn to draw water!

Legends about the Monks Well abound, and most of the stories involve secret passageways: leading either to Childwall 'Abbey' (which never was an abbey) or Childwall Priory (which was a

[Old engraving of the Monks Well]

farmhouse near the present Fiveways junction) or the Bishop Eton Monastery (which was only established in the 1840s) or even the Rose Brewery in Picton Road! It seems likely that such legends were sparked off by Victorian children, who spotted the inlet tunnel already referred to, and the outlet pipe which would have channelled the surplus water into Wavertree Lake alongside (where the children's playground is today).

In 1834 the Select Vestry - the predecessor of the Local Board of Health - installed an iron pump at the well, to lift the water from the underground chamber. They also ordered the Constable to lock the pump during church service times on Sundays, it having been found that "women met at the well when drawing water, and stayed gossiping there". With the arrival of piped water in the 1850s, the well became redundant, and the legends began to grow! Late in the nineteenth century a stone cross - inscribed 'Deus dedit, Homo bebit' (God gives, Man drinks) in accordance with local tradition - was added to the old base.

By 1932, the site was owned by a building firm - Messrs David Roberts, Son & Co. - who had bought and demolished Monkswell House to make way for an estate of semi-detached houses. The survival of the Well appeared to be threatened, but, recognising its historic value, the firm presented it to the City Council. The structure became one of Liverpool's first Listed 'Buildings' in 1952.

THE MONKS WELL TO THE ABBEY CINEMA

Now walk along Mill Lane - so called because it was the road leading from Old Swan to the ancient Wavertree Mill off Woolton Road - past the children's playground. A few yards inside the railed enclosure can be seen a sandstone block, protruding from the grassy surface, inscribed with a crown and the letter 'S'.

[The Salisbury stone]

This 'Salisbury stone' is a reminder of the old Wavertree Lake which existed on this site until 1929, and of a dispute between the Local Board and the Lord of the Manor as long ago as 1861. The Lake was a valued local asset; the existence of a water supply - springing from the original well - was probably the reason why a village developed here, the name 'Wavertree' having been translated by one scholar as "the place by the common pond". During the nineteenth century, however, it became very dirty and weed-infested, and the Local Board of Health decided to clean it up and plant trees round the edge. This provoked a reaction from the Marquess of Salisbury - Lord of the Manor of Wavertree - who ordered 'mere stones' (boundary markers) to be placed round the edge to show that it was his property rather than common land. Eventually the dispute was resolved - the Marquess agreeing to allow the Board to continue with its scheme - but one of the stones remains to this day.

Wavertree Lake was a favourite spot with local youngsters and their fishing-nets, but by the 1920s it had come to be regarded by the authorities as a source of danger rather than a source of fun. In 1929 it was filled in, the deciding factor being the need to widen Mill Lane to take electric trams. Today the only reminder - apart from the Salisbury stone and numerous surviving picture postcards - is the name Lake Road which is still officially attached to the stretch of road linking Mill Lane with the Picton Clock.

Follow the railings round into Lake Road and - watching for traffic speeding towards you from the right - cross to the triangular green on the other side. In the middle of the green stands the old Lock-up, built in 1796 for the accommodation of drunks and other prisoners overnight. This small sandstone building - now regarded as a picturesque local landmark - was objected to, at the time, by Mr John Myers, the wealthy owner of Lake House, who felt that the scheme "showed a desire to annoy him". His complaints were, however, overruled by the other villagers, who were finding the payment of board-and-lodging expenses to the local Constable an expensive business. The Constable was apparently entitled to two shillings a night (10 pence in today's money, but worth a lot more then!) for accommodating prisoners in his own house. The original cost of the Lock-up is not recorded, but it was obviously considered a worthwhile investment.

When it was first built, the Lock-up (or 'Round House' as it was commonly known, in spite of its octagonal shape) had an almost-flat roof. It was not unknown for prisoners to escape, aided by friends who hid behind the parapet and knocked a hole in the

roof after nightfall. The present pointed roof, complete with weather-vane, was added in 1869, when James Picton was commissioned by the Local Board to restore and 'beautify' the building.

The Lock-up had, in fact, become redundant for its original purpose as long ago as 1845, when the village's first Police Station was opened. It was occasionally used to isolate cholera victims from the rest of the community, and there are records of destitute Irish families having been temporarily housed in it while trekking inland from Liverpool during the famine years. Later it was used to store the village fire hose, but by the 1860s it had fallen into decay, and only Picton's interest as an architect and historian saved it from demolition. The Lock-up was made a Listed Building in 1952. The only other surviving example of such a structure in the Liverpool area is on the old Everton village green: the 'stone jug' which is featured on the badge of Everton Football Club.

The triangular green on which Wavertree's Lock-up stands is also the only surviving piece of common land in Liverpool. When the official register was compiled in 1983, all claims in respect of other areas within the City boundary were rejected by the

Government inspector. This green is, in fact, the last vestige of the much larger Wavertree Green which was 'enclosed' (divided up into fields) by Act of Parliament in 1768.

The Wavertree Enclosure Act of 1768 was promoted by the leading local landowners and tenants: in particular by the Lord of the Manor, Mr Bamber Gascoyne. This man - a distant relative of the twentieth century TV quizmaster - had acquired Wavertree (along with Childwall, Everton, West Derby and other manors) through marrying Mary Greene, the heiress of Isaac Greene who had originally purchased the various titles and lands.

The Act refers to 'Several Commons and Waste Grounds within the Manor of Wavertree' and the object of enclosure - as in other parts of the country where it was being carried out - was to increase the productivity of the land. Each new field was allotted to a named individual, who then had a direct financial incentive to apply manure and grow crops.

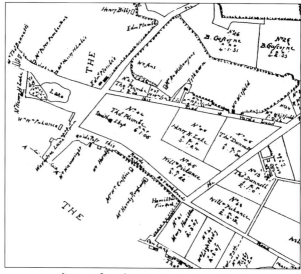

[Extract from the Wavertree Enclosure Map]

One provision of the Enclosure Act was a ban on the erection of buildings - or indeed walls over 4ft 6ins in height - on Wavertree Green. This was to leave the sails of Wavertree Mill exposed to the wind, and so to protect the interests of Bamber Gascoyne as the mill's owner. As recently as the 1930s - when plans were drawn up for what became the Abbey Cinema (now the Gala bingo club and Somerfield supermarket) - attempts were made by local residents to have this clause enforced, but their pleas were rejected by the courts on the grounds that the mill no longer existed!

Now walk away from the Lock-up, in the direction of the Picton Clock. Cross the road by means of the zebra crossing, towards the former cinema building. The 'Abbey' first opened its doors in March 1939 with 'Joy of Living', and closed down in August 1979 with 'The Towering Inferno'. It was the only cinema of that name in the Liverpool area, and gave further credence to the stories about the Monks Well. However, the reason for the name was quite simple: it was to secure the new cinema a place at the head of the alphabetical list of Merseyside cinemas, in front of the Aintree Palace, the Astoria and the Atlas!

Walk to the right, alongside the perimeter wall. The cinema's architect was A. Ernest Shennan - an Alderman on the City Council - and it was a typical example of contemporary design. Although the original windows and doors have all been replaced, it is still recognisably a thirties-style cinema building.

SECTION 9:

THE ABBEY CINEMA TO THE BLUE COAT SCHOOL

Stop opposite Waterloo Street: by the pedestrian entrance to the supermarket car park. On the other side of Church Road North is a range of buildings which can be recognised on 150-year-old maps of Wavertree. Jenkins' funeral directors' business occupies 'White Cottage' - so named on the very earliest Ordnance Survey map of the district, published in 1851 - which (though much altered) is traditionally regarded as the oldest building in Wavertree. Certainly the remnants of a sandstone wall fronting on to Waterloo Street look very ancient indeed. To the left of Waterloo Street, next door to the Coffee House pub, is a row of three brick cottages. The two on the corner (Nos 8 and 10) were knocked together and largely rebuilt in 1984 by Merseyside Improved Houses. The small enclosure in front of them is a relic of the much larger cobbled forecourt which once extended across the frontage of the pub.

[Ordnance Survey map of the Church Road North area, circa 1849]

The Coffee House itself is probably Wavertree's oldest surviving pub. The Ale House Recognizances for 1777, which are stored in the Lancashire Record Office, list just three inns in Wavertree: the Coffee House (licensee Elizabeth Heys), The Lamb (John Leech) and The Letters (Mary Plumbe). The Coffee House is probably the "good Inn and Tavern" referred to in Moss's Liverpool Guide of 1796, "where regular Assemblies are supported, in the summer season, composed of the neighbourhood and company from the town". Its Assembly Room was the venue for the inaugural meeting of the Wavertree Local Board of Health in 1851. Behind the pub was a brewery - the 'Crown Brewery' - reached through an archway (now filled in) a few yards to the left of the front door.

Just as the Lamb was the base for Dilworth's horse buses, so the Coffee House was the terminus of Joseph Mattinson's rival service. Later on the horse tram tracks from Liverpool finished right outside. In 1885 a local resident complained to the Local Board about the "nuisance ... caused by the Company's servants sweeping the refuse out of the tramcars on to the Road", proving that the litter problem is nothing new. (There were also regular reports in the 1880s and 1890s of vandalism to the Picton Clock and its lamps).

Undoubtedly the Coffee House was a very popular venue for a day excursion from Liverpool. It looked across at open fields which later became the White Star Line's sports ground. The pub was owned by Robert Cain & Sons - one of Liverpool's leading brewers - by 1900, and the sumptuous ground floor interior (since modified) was the work of their architect Walter Thomas, famous as the designer of city centre pubs such as the Philharmonic in Hope Street and the Vines in Lime Street.

[No.28 Church Road North]

Now walk along Church Road North, across the end of
the road called Wavertree Green (a 1930s revival of the
name of the old common). On the opposite side of
Church Road North, just to the left of Hunters Lane,
the Liverpool Progressive Synagogue occupies the old
Wavertree Rectory, which began life as an ordinary
house in the mid eighteenth century. This must have
been one of the first large houses to have been built in
the neighbourhood to cater for the needs of
middle-class 'immigrants' from Liverpool. It is a typical
Georgian building, standing in its own grounds and
with a short but sweeping driveway from the road. In
the 1820s the owner seems to have been 'Benjamin
Bromfield, gent.', while the 1851 Census records
Alexander Sleigh - a 'cotton and general produce
broker' born in Newcastle-under-Lyme, Staffs - his wife
Jane and their four young children, together with a
nurse, a cook and a housemaid.

Continue along Church Road North, until you are
standing opposite a pair of tall, ornamental metal
gates set between stone piers, about 100 yards before
the traffic lights. This was at one time the main
pedestrian entrance to Wavertree Hall (or 'Hamilton

Hall' as it is referred to on the 1851 Ordnance Survey map), an old mansion whose site is now occupied by the Royal School for the Blind. The 'gates' are, in fact, incapable of being opened. They were installed in 1986 as a reminder of the similarly-ornate gates which stood here until they rusted away and were removed in 1955. Through those gates, it was said, the daughter of the house had eloped with the coachman one night, and as a result her father, in sadness and disgust, had ordered them to be permanently locked. So it was that, from the mid-nineteenth century onwards, that entrance to Wavertree Hall was never used; and the present 'phoney' gates continue that tradition!

[The old gates of Wavertree Hall]

The School for the Blind building dates from 1898, having been paid for largely by an anonymous donor (thought to have been Miss Mary Louisa Hornby, a cousin of the Hornby sisters of Sandown Hall). The architects were Messrs H. & A. P. Fry of Liverpool. The old Wavertree Hall - not, it seems, considered at the time to be a building of any great interest - was completely demolished to make way for it. The Liverpool School for the Blind had been founded in Commutation Row, by Edward Rushton, as long ago as 1791. It was the first school of its type in Britain - second only to one in Paris - and by the 1890s was well-established in Hardman Street, Liverpool. The Elementary Education (Blind and Deaf Children) Act of 1893 made a new building necessary, and the Wavertree site was decided upon. The 'Royal' prefix was authorised by the Queen in 1966.

Now cross Woolton Road, at the traffic lights, and continue along Church Road. Across the road is the Church of Holy Trinity - dating from 1794 and

described by the late Sir John Betjeman as "Liverpool's best Georgian church". On your left is the church hall. Stop at the far end of the church hall, where you will see some stone steps alongside the pavement. This is the so-called 'mounting stone' - used in the nineteenth century by churchgoers to get back in the saddle after services - which used to stand on the other side of the road. Its shape and well-worn steps suggest, however, that it may have originated

[The mounting stone, Church Road]

as a field stile long before the church was built.

The date of Holy Trinity Church is significant. The 1790s were the decade when the wealthy merchants of Liverpool began to take a real interest in villages like Wavertree as places in which to live. Until it was built, the nearest church was All Saints Childwall, whose parish extended all the way from Wavertree to Speke. In fact Holy Trinity was a Chapel of Ease to Childwall until 1867, when it finally became a parish church in its own right. John Hope's original design for Holy

Trinity included a stone 'lantern' on the tower at the far end, which made the building a prominent landmark. This survived into the twentieth century, but unfortunately had to be taken down for safety reasons. In 1911 the east end of the church (nearest the road) was skilfully remodelled in 'neo-Grec' style by Charles Reilly, who was a friend of the then Rector. Reilly was Professor of Architecture at Liverpool University.

[Holy Trinity Church as it was when first built]

Continue walking along Church Road until you reach the corner of Bristol Road, opposite the gates of the Blue Coat School. The imposing School building - described as 'spectacular' by the late Prof. Nikolaus Pevsner - was designed by the Liverpool partnership Briggs, Wolstenholme & Thornely, perhaps best-known as the architects of the Dock Office at the Pier Head. It was opened in 1906 - when the pupils were transferred from the old building in School Lane, Liverpool - and the clock tower was added in 1915. The very impressive Chapel - the large domed building to the left of the main school - was designed by the same architects, having been paid for by Mr T. Fenwick-Harrison (of the Harrison shipping line) as a memorial to his late wife. Like the neighbouring Holy Trinity Church, the school and its chapel are both Grade II* ('two starred') Listed Buildings: i.e. classed as 'particularly important' in the national context.

The Liverpool Blue Coat School - or Blue Coat Hospital, to give it its original title - was founded in 1708 by Mr Bryan Blundell and Rev. Robert Styth as "a school for teaching poor children to read, write and cast accounts". Blundell was a leading Liverpool shipowner - reputedly the owner of the first ship to enter the town's first dock in 1715 - and slave trader, participating in the 'triangular trade' which linked Liverpool, West Africa and the Caribbean. Styth was the first joint Rector of Liverpool, based at St Nicholas Church on the waterfront. Both men were aware of the problems of orphan children in Liverpool, large numbers of whom were left destitute by the loss of their fathers at sea.

The original school expanded rapidly and a new building (the present Bluecoat Chambers in School Lane) was opened in 1718. It was still in use in 1899, when the decision to move 'to the countryside' was made and the land here in Church Road - overlooking the newly-opened Wavertree Playground - was purchased.

The Blue Coat School retained its 'orphanage' role until the late 1940s, the boys and girls in their old-fashioned dress having been a familiar sight in Wavertree during the interwar years. In 1949, however, it became a 'secondary bilateral' school for boys only (day pupils as well as boarders). Girls were re-admitted - though to the sixth form only - in 1990, when the boarding house eventually closed owing to lack of demand. In 1997 - after several years as a nominally comprehensive school - the Blue Coat changed its status once again, becoming a Grant Maintained School selecting its pupils on the basis of academic ability.

THE BLUE COAT SCHOOL TO THE MILL SITE

Directly opposite the school, on the side of Church Road where you are currently standing, is another very impressive Edwardian building: a block of three huge, gabled houses standing between Bristol Road and Hereford Road. Officially named Dovercourt or Tudor House, this block was known to older residents of the area as 'Dilworth's Folly'.

[Dilworth's Folly, Church Road]

The story goes that - when the Blue Coat School purchased its Wavertree site - two local builders, Isaac Dilworth and Charles Berrington, were determined to bid for the contract. Never having built a school before, however, they had to establish their credentials, and the way they did it was to build these huge houses facing directly across to the proposed school site. The materials used were the same as those specified for the school - red brick and green slates, with white glazed tiles used inside the wash-houses at the back - and one of the houses is said to have incorporated a sprung maple dance floor! Sad to say,

Dilworth and Berrington failed to win the contract for the school, which went instead to Messrs Morrison & Sons, the Wavertree building firm which was also the main contractor for Liverpool's Anglican Cathedral. Dilworth himself moved into Tudor House, and died there in 1909.

Now turn into Hereford Road (the next turning on the left) opposite the school Chapel. Walk uphill, away from Church Road. The 'bye-law' houses here are much more conventional, in terms both of size and style. Gore's Liverpool Directory for 1913 lists a teacher of music at No.1 Hereford Road, a secretary at No.3, and master mariners at Nos 5 and 7, the road's other residents including a draughtsman, a pawnbroker's assistant, a sculptor and a wine dealer.

Stop at the top of Hereford Road, where it meets Charles Berrington Road. All the roads on this estate - with the exception of Charles Berrington Road itself - were named after cathedrals or minsters: Peterborough, Hereford, Lichfield, Newcastle, etc. The reason for this was that Berrington's cousin - and foreman joiner - was Charles Litchfield, whose name therefore inspired not just one but nine separate street names!

Now walk to the left along Charles Berrington Road. It is unusual for the name of a builder to be commemorated in such a direct way: such lengthy street names more usually referring to political or similar personalities. Apparently the less-ostentatious name 'Berrington Road' was originally suggested, but vetoed by the Council because of possible confusion with Barrington Road which is not far away.

Charles Berrington was born in Bedfordshire in 1848. His mother was a lacemaker, and the travellers who took the finished pieces in exchange for more cotton told tales of Liverpool where the streets were 'paved with gold'. Charles's opportunity to visit the city came when one of his nephews decided to emigrate to America. Using horses and a wagon borrowed from the family farm, Charles gave him a lift to the docks, probably intending to return with goods for sale. Having arrived in Liverpool, however, Charles found the business opportunities irresistible, and set up as a teamster and stevedore in Toxteth.

His move into house-building came in the 1890s. It was unusual for an Englishman to break into this Welsh-dominated industry, but Berrington was perhaps inspired by the contrast between the Liverpool slums and the 'model' village of Cardington where he had grown up. After building in the Aigburth district, he acquired this Heathfield Park estate, between Church Road and Heathfield Road, and established a builder's yard in Woolton Road nearby.

The last house on the right-hand side of Charles Berrington Road - No.66, which at one time had a wooden balcony - is listed in old street directories as the 'Heathfield Park Estate Office', owned by the Executors of Charles Berrington. This is a reminder that, when they were first built, the houses were all rented; owner occupation being very uncommon in Liverpool before the 1930s. Berrington himself died in Bedford in 1910, leaving assets valued at over £330,000. (Isaac Dilworth, by comparison, had left only £5,000).

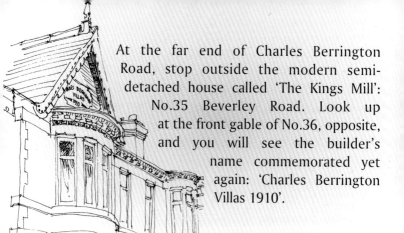

At the far end of Charles Berrington Road, stop outside the modern semi-detached house called 'The Kings Mill': No.35 Beverley Road. Look up at the front gable of No.36, opposite, and you will see the builder's name commemorated yet again: 'Charles Berrington Villas 1910'.

[Charles Berrington Villas, Beverley Road]

You are now standing near one of the most historic spots in Wavertree: the site of Wavertree Mill. Beverley Road is marked on the Wavertree Enclosure Map of 1769 as an unnamed trackway leading from the present-day Church Road (before the church was built) to what was, even then, regarded as an ancient windmill site. The mill itself stood just behind the pair of modern semis: Nos 35 and 37 Beverley Road. These houses were built in 1986 after the City Council granted planning permission for the mill's remains to be swept away. A vigorous campaign by the Wavertree Society failed to prevent the development, though it did result in a thorough archaeological investigation of the site, and the relocation of some of the bricks and stone blocks from the mill's foundations. This material remains on view - in the front gardens of the modern houses - together with an old millstone which was also recovered from the site.

Numerous photographs exist of Wavertree Mill in varying states of dereliction, prior to its demolition in 1916. It was a 'post mill', consisting of a circular brick base and an unusually-shaped timber superstructure. The timber part, including the sails, could be turned to face the wind. It revolved around a huge central post, which was supported by four timber 'legs' hidden within the brickwork. The stone slabs which survive each supported one of these legs, and the ring of bricks indicates their position in relation to the base. A few yards out from the base was a ring of stone blocks - clearly visible in 1985, but now completely destroyed - on which ran a large cartwheel attached to the end of a wooden pole. This pole projected from the body of the mill, and was the means by which it was turned round.

[Old postcard view of Wavertree Mill and Quarry]

In spite of all the surrounding housing development, and the fact that the remains of the mill have been moved some 15 yards, it is still possible to appreciate why this site was chosen in medieval times for what was one of only four 'Kings Mills' in the Liverpool area. The ground slopes away in all directions, ensuring a good flow of wind to the sails. Records indicate the existence of a mill here as long ago as 1452 - a document of 1475 refers to a "mill called Watremylne" - and for almost 200 years it was the property of the Crown. In 1639 Charles I granted it, along with the Township of Wavertree, to Lord Strange, son of the Earl of Derby. Wavertree Mill was valuable property, for it carried with it the power of 'soke': that is the power to seize the produce, or the cart and horses, of any local farmer who refused to bring his corn here to be ground.

By the eighteenth century - which was the estimated date of the remains uncovered by the archaeological dig - the mill had passed into the hands of the Lord of the Manor, Mr Bamber Gascoyne, who lived at Childwall Hall. The Wavertree Enclosure Act of 1768 prohibited the erection of any house or building, or the planting of any trees or the growth of any existing trees, within 200 yards of the mill "to such a height as to prevent the going of the said windmill". In the nineteenth century this caused problems for Col. James Bourne of Heathfield - the mansion whose grounds were later to be developed by Charles Berrington - for he was very keen on trees and liberally planted them around the perimeter of his estate. Threatened with legal action by the Marquess of Salisbury - Bamber Gascoyne's successor - Col. Bourne eventually decided to lease the mill himself in order to avoid having to cut down his trees.

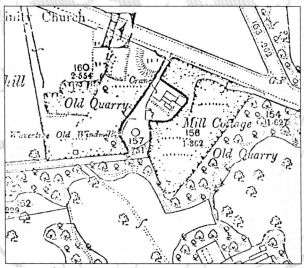

[The Woolton Road area circa 1891, as shown on the Ordnance Survey 1:2500 scale map]

THE MILL SITE TO CHILDWALL ROAD

Now walk along the narrow public footpath sandwiched between the modern houses and the older (1930s) houses in Beverley Road. This is a very ancient right of way. In 1867 Col. Bourne (whose wealth was derived from coal mines in the St Helens area) wrote to the Local Board, asking for the finger-posts indicating this path to be removed, claiming that "it is simply the resort of idle boys and men, anxious to avoid observation, more especially on Sundays". His request was agreed to, but "without prejudice to the footpath being the property of the Township"; and the path survives to this day. At the other end the path opens out into what was once the main approach to the mill from Woolton Road. On the right is a pair of semi-detached cottages, still called Mill Cottages. Either side of the mill access road are small estates of typical 1930s semis - Tor View Road to the left and Mendip Road to the right - which mark the sites of two large quarries. Sandstone was taken from here from the late eighteenth century onwards - the Enclosure Map includes the words 'left for stone' to the east of the mill - leaving the windmill standing on a narrow isthmus of rock.

The quarry on the site of the present Mendip Road was the Township Quarry for Wavertree. This is where the yellowish stone probably came from for the construction of Holy Trinity Church and the Lock-up, as well as field-boundary walls. Later on - when it became exhausted - the quarry was used as a pound for keeping stray cattle and other animals. Eventually it became a tip for household refuse. Older residents of the area still remember the site of Tor View Road -

across the way from Mill Cottages - as the 'Bin Field', which is a reminder that the second quarry was also filled-in in this way, starting late in the nineteenth century. Domestic waste in those days - before the age of plastic wrappers and gas central heating - consisted largely of ashes, so by the 1930s both former quarries were considered suitable for house-building.

[Old postcard view of Wavertree Mill, looking up from Woolton Road]

The windmill itself is said to have ceased regular operation in 1873, but seems to have worked intermittently until 1890, when the final lease from the Marquess of Salisbury expired. Severe gales in 1895 wrecked the sails and damaged the structure beyond repair, but it was 1916 before the decaying skeleton was finally pulled down. After that, the area became the site of lock-up garages; laid out in a crescent (backing on to the old public footpath) so as to leave the mill's foundations exposed. After nearly seventy more years as a local talking-point, regularly visited by groups of schoolchildren studying local history, the site was finally obliterated in 1986.

During the Victorian era, Wavertree Mill was widely regarded as being jinxed. In July 1866, ten-year-old Richard Matthews died after being struck by the sails of the windmill. His father (also called Richard) was Col. Bourne's coachman. Some years later, the sails caught the hair of Charles Taylor's eldest daughter. The local historian James Hoult tells us that "she was scalped and was rendered insensible for twelve hours, but happily she recovered". Rumour spread that the old quarry was inhabited by an evil spirit. Eventually, it is said, the miller took the advice he was given, and set the sails in such a way as their shadow formed a cross touching all four corners of the quarry. No more accidents are recorded after that!

Walk down the trackway - the original cinders and bare sandstone now hidden under tarmac and concrete - on to Woolton Road, and turn right. Woolton Road is a long, straight thoroughfare dating back over 200 years. The Enclosure Map calls it "the Road from Hamiltons Fir Nook towards Gateacre"; Mrs Margaret Hamilton having owned the land (in Fir Lane) which later became Holy Trinity churchyard. Cross Woolton Road when it is safe to do so, and continue walking to the right until you reach the corner of Lance Lane. The stone wall bordering the playing-fields was presumably considered low enough to comply with the terms of the Wavertree Enclosure Act, though a smithy which once stood in this vicinity was ordered to be removed. St Stephen's United Reformed Church, on the opposite corner of Woolton Road, was originally built in 1929 by the Presbyterian Church of England.

Turn left into Lance Lane, named after Thomas Lance (1769-1829) an insurance broker who owned property here. Walk alongside the playing-field fence until you are opposite the new Medical Centre, beyond Tulip Road. Cross the road at this point, and continue walking until you reach the end of Lance Grove. The Wavertree Enclosure Map of 1769 shows a small group of buildings here, including a 'Tyth Barn' set back from the road and reached by means of a trackway, but none of these buildings appears to have survived into the twentieth century.

The old Cenacle Convent, situated just beyond Lance Grove, was demolished in 1991 to make way for a new private housing estate. The convent had been built about 1910 on the site of The Elms, a large Georgian mansion.

Walk along Lance Lane past this estate, which - at the suggestion of the Wavertree Society - has been given the name Tithebarn Grove. When the new houses were built, efforts were made to retain as many as possible of the mature trees which were such a feature of the site. The fifty which survived are now the subject of a Tree Preservation Order. At the end of Lance Lane, cross the dual carriageway of Childwall Road at the traffic lights, and turn right. Looking across Childwall Road, you will see a terrace of three large houses at right-angles to the road, including the Wonderland day nursery.

This terrace - with its tall gables, roughcast walls and small-paned casement windows - must have looked very contemporary in 1899, when it was built. The architect - who was clearly influenced by the Arts and Crafts Movement - may have been Thomas Edgar Eccles, from Roby, who was to become president of the Liverpool Architectural Society in 1908. His brother, the coal agent J. Heron Eccles, was the first occupant of the house furthest from the road ('The Poplars') which is actually numbered 1a Lance Lane. This house was also the home, between 1980 and 1982, of Alan Bleasdale, the famous Liverpool playwright. It was here that he wrote 'The Boys from the Blackstuff'.

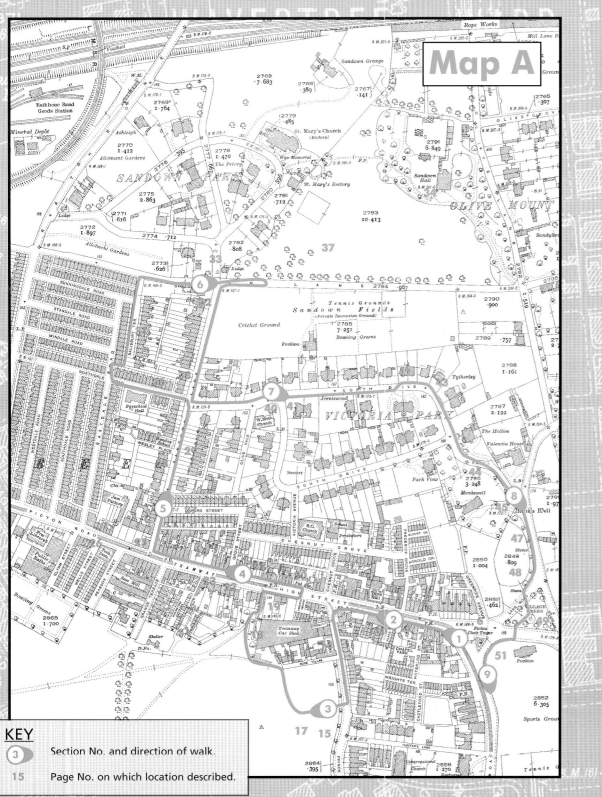

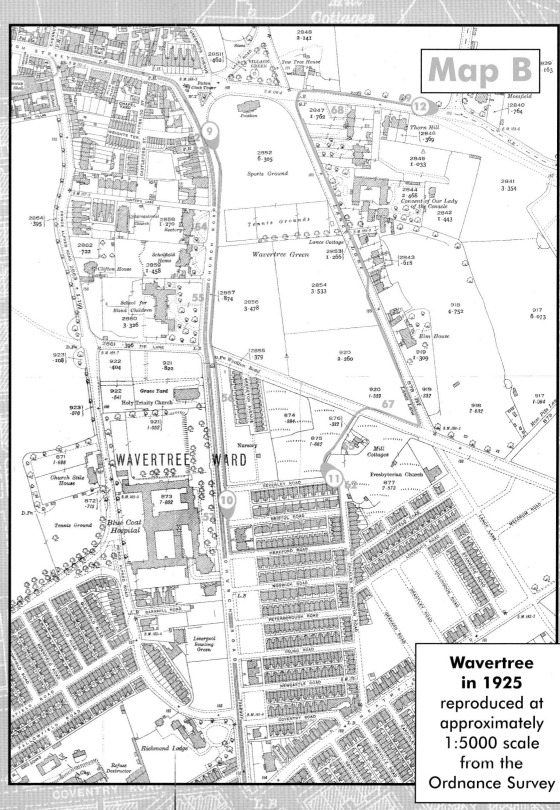

Map A

Map B

Wavertree in 1925
reproduced at approximately 1:5000 scale from the Ordnance Survey

Now walk along Childwall Road, following the long sandstone wall behind which is the Olive Mount Wing of Childwall Comprehensive School (originally opened as Olive Mount Secondary Modern in 1951). The dual carriageway was laid out in the 1930s along the line of an earlier road: named as 'Moss Pit Lane' on the 1851 Ordnance Survey map as it ran towards Childwall across marshy ground. Walk past the school entrance, and stop about 20 yards before the next road junction.

A careful examination of the wall at this point will reveal two unusual stones - six courses up from the ground, and 40 feet apart - each carved with a row of four horseshoes. Wavertree folklore says that 'this is where the horse thieves were hanged', or alternatively (and less dramatically) that 'Shacklady's Smithy once stood near here'. Perhaps the stones are relics of the old smithy on Wavertree Green, demolished as a result of the Enclosure Act?

[The horseshoe stones, Childwall Road]

CHILDWALL ROAD TO SOUTHWAY

When you have managed to locate the horseshoe stones, continue walking alongside the wall, and stop on the corner. On the other corner of Thingwall Road is 'Mossfield' - now a Council-run children's home - which, at the time of the 1861 Census, was the residence of Dr James Kenyon (formerly of the High Street) his wife, five children and three servants (cook, nurse and housemaid). It is one of a small group of villas - the others being 'Nos.1, 2 and 3 Thornhill', on the opposite side of Childwall Road - built here, overlooking open countryside, in the mid-nineteenth century.

Now walk along Thingwall Road, keeping the sandstone wall on your left. In the nineteenth century this wall was the boundary of the Olive Mount estate. Olive Mount was a Georgian mansion which set the pattern for a whole series of similar houses, standing in their own grounds, forming a virtual ring around the old village of Wavertree: Sandown Hall, Westdale House and The Grange being other examples. Close to the point where the road bears round to the right was an ornamental lake (marked as a 'fish pond' on the 1893 Ordnance Survey map).

Continue on Thingwall Road, walking alongside the Manweb sports ground. Between the tower blocks of Olive Mount Heights and the Manweb club-house you will see a red-brick building: a former school, now the Art Annexe of Childwall Comprehensive. This building is all that survives of the Wavertree Cottage Homes complex, built in the grounds of Olive Mount at the very end of the nineteenth century. Just a few yards further along - from opposite No.78 Thingwall Road - you should be able to catch a glimpse of the mansion itself: immediately to the right of Olive Mount Heights.

[Olive Mount]

Olive Mount - the mansion - seems to have been built in the early 1790s for Mr James Swan. Swan was a grocer and tea dealer who had business premises in Castle Street, Liverpool, and who in 1790 had lived very close by in Redcross Street (between the present Derby Square and the river). Gore's Liverpool Directory for 1796 lists him for the first time as living in Wavertree. He was then 47 years old, and business was obviously going well. Whether Swan's new house gave its name to the hill on which it stood, or vice versa, we do not know, but he must have chosen this spot - one of the highest points in the vicinity of Liverpool - for its elevated position and views across the open countryside. The house is typically Georgian in style, and built of local cream sandstone.

James Swan died, aged 80 years, in 1829. The house was put up for sale, and at the time of the 1841 Census it was the residence of 50 year old Luke Thomas Crossley, who was described as 'Independent' (i.e. not working for a living) and born outside Lancashire. Living with him at Olive Mount were his wife, their six daughters (aged 5-14) and five servants.

By 1861 the Crossleys had moved away, and the house was occupied by Adam Steuart Gladstone, an East India merchant who was a cousin of the famous Liverpool-born Prime Minister. By 1871 Francis Hollins, a cotton broker, had arrived. And by 1881 Olive Mount was the home of another merchant: Thomas Dyson Hornby, the nephew of Hugh Hornby of Sandown Hall. Then in 1897 the estate was purchased by the Liverpool Select Vestry, for the building of Cottage Homes.

The Liverpool Select Vestry was part of the Victorian Poor Law system. It administered the giant Liverpool Workhouse on Brownlow Hill (where the Roman Catholic Cathedral stands today). In 1889 the West Derby Union - which was the body responsible for Poor Law administration on the out-skirts of Liverpool, including Wavertree - had opened Cottage Homes at Fazakerley, the first of their kind in Britain. These Homes aimed to give orphans and other destitute children the sense of belonging to a 'family' group, rather than a vast and impersonal institution. The experiment was obviously a success, for the Liverpool Select Vestry decided to copy the West Derby example and in 1901 established its own Cottage Homes here at Olive Mount.

Eventually, in 1925, the two Poor Law bodies were amalgamated. The Wavertree Cottage Homes were then used only for children up to the age of seven, older children being accommodated at Fazakerley. When the Poor Law was abolished, the Olive Mount estate became a Children's Hospital, which in later years specialised in the care of the mentally handicapped. With the advent of 'care in the community' it closed down, and virtually all of the buildings were demolished in 1991. The original house - which had been used as the administrative centre of the hospital - was retained by the Health Authority as offices. Dwarfed and overshadowed by the three thirteen-storey blocks of flats - built just yards away from its front door in 1963, before it became a Listed Building - the mansion has lost its original privacy, and its view, but it remains a fine example of a Georgian merchant's residence.

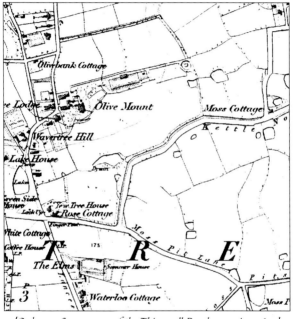

[Ordnance Survey map of the Thingwall Road area, circa 1849]

Continue walking along Thingwall Road. Prior to 1906 this was called 'Broad Green Road', and on the Ordnance Survey map published in 1851 it is labelled 'Kettle Nook'. Its meandering course is also instantly recognisable on the Wavertree Enclosure Map, drawn in 1769. This was one of the few pre-existing roads in the area at that time: one of the 'rolling English roads made by the rolling English drunkard' to misquote G. K. Chesterton.

Outside No.103 Thingwall Road, a circular green plate on a lamp-post announces that you are entering the Wavertree Garden Suburb Conservation Area. In 1974 the City Planning Officer described this area as "a community in a garden ... an important example of good civic design and town planning" the character of which it was desirable to preserve. The Liverpool Garden Suburb - as it was originally called - was in fact one of only twenty or so similar developments planned and built up and down the country in the decade prior to the First World War. The fact that it remains today a popular and attractive place to live is a clear indication of the far-sightedness of its founders.

Only the houses on the left-hand side of Thingwall Road, at this point, were part of the original Garden Suburb. The semi-detached houses on the right-hand side of the road came 25 years later, in the 1930s, but the influence of the Garden Suburb architects on subsequent housing design is obvious. The semis are typical of the private housing built on the edge of Liverpool - and, indeed, other British towns and cities - between the wars, but quite a contrast to the 'bye-law' terraces which were the norm prior to 1918.

How did this change in fashion come about? Why did red brick and slate give way to pebbledash and tile? Why was this corner of Wavertree chosen for the Garden Suburb experiment in 1910? Who were the promoters, the designers, and the early inhabitants? The story of Wavertree Garden Suburb is part of our national, and not just local, history. Turn the corner into Southway and try to imagine yourself back in the days before the First World War, when the residents regarded themselves, with good reason, as 'the pioneers'!

SOUTHWAY TO WAVERTREE NOOK ROAD

Wavertree Garden Suburb was a co-partnership housing scheme. This means that the houses were owned neither individually nor by a profit-seeking private landlord. The owner of the whole estate was a company called Liverpool Garden Suburb Tenants Ltd, in which the tenants of the houses were themselves shareholders. (You can still see the initials L.G.S.T. on manhole covers and rainwater heads all over the estate). Shares could also be purchased by outsiders, the annual dividend generally being limited to five per cent. Since the tenants had a financial interest in the estate, it was assumed that repair costs would be kept down, and investment in the company would literally be 'as safe as houses'.

[Garden Suburb rainwater head]

There was a touch of crusading zeal about the company. "The object", said the initial prospectus, "is to provide a residential suburb for the people of Liverpool amid surroundings which conduce to both health and pleasure". Its telegraphic address was 'Antislum, Liverpool'. The intention was always to plough back a proportion of the profits to pay for the further expansion of the estate.

The idea of building a Garden Suburb here came not from Liverpool but from London. Henry Vivian - the first Chairman of Liverpool Garden Suburb Tenants Ltd - was also Chairman of

[Henry Vivian 1868-1930]

Co-partnership Tenants Ltd, a London-based organisation dedicated to establishing Garden Suburbs all over the country. He was a carpenter by background, an active trade unionist who did not see why the ordinary working man should not share in the profits of house ownership. He set up the very first co-partnership housing scheme - Ealing Tenants Ltd - in west London in 1901, and by the time L.G.S.T. was established in 1910 there were eleven similar companies in operation in towns as diverse as Stoke-on-Trent, Keswick (Cumbria) and Sevenoaks (Kent). Vivian had become an M.P. in 1906, having been elected as the Liberal member for Birkenhead.

The first houses on the Ealing estate were not 'garden suburb' type houses at all. They were redbrick terraces, very similar to the sort being built (by speculative individuals and companies) in Liverpool at that time. It was Vivian's political friendship with Ralph Neville, Chairman of The First Garden City Company Ltd at Letchworth, that persuaded him to advocate low-density planning for all the subsequent co-partnership estates, including Wavertree.

Southway was originally called North Way, but was renamed in the 1920s following the building of council houses further along the road. Walk along the left-hand side until you reach No.10. The extra-wide garden at the side of this house was a bone of contention between L.G.S.T. and the City Council when the estate was first laid out. On the original plans it is shown as a side road, but the company had no intention of ever building one. The reason for including it was that the Liverpool Corporation (Streets and Buildings) Act of 1908 required an intersecting street every 150 yards, in order to ensure the circulation of air around long terraces. The Council decided that no concession could be made in this case, even though the overall density of the estate was only 11 houses to the acre, rather than the 40 to the acre which was normal in Liverpool at the time.

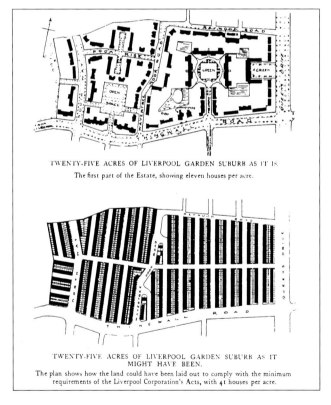

TWENTY-FIVE ACRES OF LIVERPOOL GARDEN SUBURB AS IT IS.
The first part of the Estate, showing eleven houses per acre.

TWENTY-FIVE ACRES OF LIVERPOOL GARDEN SUBURB AS IT MIGHT HAVE BEEN.
The plan shows how the land could have been laid out to comply with the minimum requirements of the Liverpool Corporation's Acts, with 41 houses per acre.

[Twenty-five acres 'as it might have been', 1914]

Now cross over Southway and continue walking away from Thingwall Road. Stop on the next corner, which is Nook Rise. Already you will have noticed that while the houses have certain features in common - like the small-paned windows - there are variations in design. The 'monotony' of traditional terraces was something the architects consciously strove to avoid. At the same time, building costs were kept down by purchasing bricks, tiles and windows in bulk, and transporting them to the various co-partnership estates around the country by rail.

The architecture of the Garden Suburb was strongly influenced by the cottage architecture of southern England. In fact the bricks and tiles were manufactured (by a co-operative firm) in Letchworth Garden City, Hertfordshire, and it was Letchworth - founded in 1903 - that had set the architectural pattern for co-partnership housing schemes all over England.

Because of the similarity with Letchworth, many people referred to the Wavertree estate, in the early days, as a 'Garden City', but this was very definitely a misnomer. For true Garden Cities were the idea of a housing reformer called Ebenezer Howard. He had visited 'model' industrial villages like Cadbury's Bournville (in Birmingham) and Lever's Port Sunlight (on Merseyside) and been impressed by their spacious layout and wide range of social facilities. His dream was of a series of free-standing Garden Cities - combining the benefits of town and country, but the disadvantages of neither - where the residents would have not only decent houses to live in but also recreational facilities and a choice of employers close at hand.

In the event - largely owing to the difficulty of attracting firms away from the established centres of population - only two such Garden Cities were ever established: at Letchworth and Welwyn. But other reformers, including Henry Vivian, seized the chance to build 'garden city type' housing on the edge of existing towns and cities, leaving the residents to commute to work by bus, tram and train. Ebenezer Howard was not pleased, for suburban sprawl was the very thing which he had sought to avoid.

Now turn right, into Nook Rise. The roadside trees in Southway and Nook Rise are one of the most attractive features of the estate, and those responsible for planting the saplings in 1911 would surely be very pleased to see how they have matured. In fact some of these people may still be alive today, for in Nook Rise each tree was planted and looked after by a child living nearby.

Walk along Nook Rise as far as the crossroads in the middle, where two cul-de-sacs meet. The cul-de-sac was a popular feature of Garden Suburbs, firstly because it gave a 'sense of community' to those living within it, and secondly because it saved money on road construction. Economic arguments such as this were put forward very strongly by one of the key figures in the Garden Suburb movement: Raymond Unwin, the town planner responsible for the layout of Letchworth in 1904, Hampstead Garden Suburb (probably the best-known example in England) in 1906, and this first section of Wavertree Garden Suburb in 1910.

In 1912 Unwin published an influential pamphlet called 'Nothing Gained by Overcrowding', arguing the case for low-density house-building. One of his

[Raymond Unwin
1863-1940]

principles was that recreation grounds should be hidden away behind the houses rather than laid out along road frontages, and this is well illustrated here. For at the head of the right-hand cul-de-sac is a gate leading to the Suburb's bowling green and tennis courts, the existence of which is little-known except to club members and residents.

The early provision of recreational facilities was an important objective of most Garden Suburbs. Here at Wavertree, the 'Town Planning Review' was able to report, in October 1911, that: "A bowling green and two lawn tennis courts have been laid, and a gravel playground about half an acre in extent has been provided for the children and furnished with swings and see-saws".

Nowadays the bowling and tennis facilities belong to private clubs, and you should not attempt to enter the recreation area. Instead, continue walking along Nook Rise, and turn right at the end into Wavertree Nook Road.

[Wavertree Nook Road and
Nook Rise in 1911]

WAVERTREE NOOK ROAD TO THE GARDEN SUBURB INSTITUTE

Walk for about 100 yards along the right-hand side of Wavertree Nook Road, until you are outside No.13. This was the very first house to be built in the Garden Suburb, and under the bay window you can see the foundation stone laid on 20th July 1910 by the Marchioness of Salisbury. The stone-laying ceremony was attended by the Lord Mayor of Liverpool and other prominent local personalities, who were treated to a programme of entertainment by the 'Victorian Court Band' and stirring speeches by Henry Vivian and others drawing attention to the wonderful Garden Suburb that was about to be created.

The Marchioness of Salisbury was, of course, the wife of Lord Salisbury, and he too spoke of his pride in being associated with the venture. It was the Marquess who had made the land available to Liverpool Garden Suburb Tenants on what were described as 'favourable terms'. In all, 180 acres - sufficient for over 1,800 houses - had been promised, which would make this Garden Suburb the largest in the country. Initially, though, it was just the 12 acres between Wavertree Nook Road and Southway which had been taken on a 999-year lease, and for which Raymond Unwin had planned the layout.

The stone-laying ceremony - on the edge of a field from which the hay had only just been cut - was followed by rapid progress. The present No.13 Wavertree Nook Road was completed and occupied in December 1910, and shortly afterwards the other houses nearby were also occupied. It is difficult to imagine the feelings of the first residents, moving to such an isolated place, and into houses quite different from any built in Liverpool before: with gardens front and back, yet available at rents (from just under six shillings a week) similar to those being charged by the landlords of conventional terraces.

['A Birds Eye View of the Liverpool Ga Suburb', 1912: from an early publicity leafl

Inevitably, the residents of Garden Suburb housing were not a typical cross-section of 'ordinary people'. In addition to the rent, payment toward the purchase of shares in the company had to be made, and a fairly hefty down-payment was required when the tenants first moved in. Garden suburbs were not the solution to the slum problem, but the argument was that they would release housing accommodation in the areas from which the tenants came.

According to Gore's Liverpool Directory for 1913, the first 118 houses in Wavertree Garden Suburb had attracted 16 clerks, 10 printing workers, 7 schoolteachers, 5 commercial travellers, 4 joiners, 4 managers and a wide variety of other occupations including an analytical chemist, a musician, a shipwright and a tram-driver. They included some interesting characters, pen-pictures of whom were published in the residents' fortnightly magazine 'The Thingwallian'. For example at No.15 Wavertree Nook Road - then named 'Paxhaven' - lived Mr Albert Mann, the local secretary of the National Anti-Gambling League, and a supporter of the Peace Society (though in everyday life a Post Office telegraphist). Clearly, some of the early tenants were attracted by the political ideals of the Suburb's founders, though others complained (again through the columns of 'The Thingwallian') about the 'compulsory Communism' which used part of their rent to pay for recreational and other social facilities.

Now cross over Wavertree Nook Road and continue walking towards Thingwall Road. The housing layout on this side - the second phase of the Suburb's development - was the work of Co-partnership Tenants Ltd's architect, George Lister Sutcliffe. (Although a design competition had been held in 1911, and the prize awarded to Liverpool student J. N. Dixon, none of the entries was actually implemented). Todmorden-born Sutcliffe had been responsible for many of the house designs within Unwin's initial phase, as well as houses in Ealing, Letchworth and Hampstead Garden Suburb. He was clearly a very imaginative architect/planner, but was to die young - aged 51 - in 1915.

G. Lister Sutcliffe 1864-1915]

Turn left round the corner into Thingwall Road. As in Wavertree Nook Road - the meandering line of which can be recognised on old maps - the Garden Suburb's designers made a conscious effort to preserve the natural features of Thingwall Road intact. The wide grass verges were retained, and some of the houses - for example the block beginning with No.137 - were set back from the road to avoid the felling of existing trees. Walk on past this row of houses until you reach the Garden Suburb Institute.

Cottage-style housing set amid green surroundings was just one of the hallmarks of a Garden Suburb in the years leading up to the First World War. Another was the possession of an Institute: a place where the residents could socialise together, entertain and also educate themselves. Liverpool Garden Suburb Tenants Ltd had planned a large, purpose-designed Institute on Queens Drive, but although the foundation stone was laid in 1914 (roughly where St Francis Xavier's School stands today) the building never materialised. Instead, this small sandstone building on Thingwall Road - converted out of a pair of cottages in 1912 for use as the Suburb's 'Temporary Club House' - is still in use today.

[*The Garden Suburb Institute*]

The Institute was the meeting-place of clubs and societies such as the Billiards Club, the Choral Society, the Horticultural Society, the Juniors Club, the Magazine Club, the Parliamentary Debating Society and the Women's Guild. It was (as it still is) the venue for concerts and plays, including - 'The Thingwallian' reported in 1914 - "the wonderful and weird production, entitled 'The Suburb in 2001 AD', in which play Messrs Mann and Faulkner appeared as the completely emancipated women of that period"! Henry Vivian and others gave lectures there, on the merits of Garden Suburb life. In addition the Institute was the meeting-place of the Tenants' Council: a group of representatives elected street by street to pass on tenants' views and complaints to the Board of Management.

Already, by the time the 200th house was completed in 1913, the fame of Wavertree Garden Suburb was spreading. Publications such as the 'Town Planning Review' - the journal of the Department of Civic Design at Liverpool University - and the national magazine 'Co-partnership' gave regular updates on the estate's progress. In October 1913 'Co-partnership' reported visits by two groups of Germans: town planners and members of a working-men's association. At the end of a musical gathering at the Institute, speeches were made and translated, and the visitors "all leaped to their feet with military precision and gave three resounding Hochs! for their English friends".

Such international get-togethers at the Institute were destined not to last. On 4th July 1914 - at the stone-laying ceremony on Queens Drive - the Lord Mayor of Liverpool said that "only in good homes, with good environment, could England produce sons and daughters with the physical and mental qualities necessary for the maintenance a great Imperial race". Exactly one month later, Britain and Germany were at war.

The First World War brought all civilian building work to a halt. It also provided a pause for thought. Raymond Unwin was appointed as the government's Chief Town Planning Inspector, and a member of the

Tudor Walters Committee, to plan Lloyd George's 'homes fit for heroes'. The result was the Housing and Town Planning Act of 1919, which established low-density, 'garden suburb' type housing as the norm and gave local authorities financial incentives to provide it. In addition, rent controls were introduced, which - combined with the effects of building cost inflation - made the co-partnership system increasingly uneconomic.

The terraced houses opposite the Institute were virtually the last to be built in Wavertree Garden Suburb. When construction ceased in 1915, 360 houses had been built out of the 1,800 originally planned. Liverpool Garden Suburb Tenants Ltd began to sell off its houses to individual owner-occupiers in the 1930s, and in 1938 the company was finally wound up, its land and remaining houses having been transferred to the (private) Conway Property Company. The undeveloped land had been sold to speculative house-builders, who proceeded to build standard-pattern semis such as those to be seen across Thingwall Road.

The tennis courts, bowling greens and the Institute were all threatened with closure, but were rescued by the Marquess of Salisbury who transferred them to a charitable Trust. Today, the Institute still functions as a social centre, though 'Saturday evening meetings of the Discussion Society' have given way to Bingo! Meanwhile, only a handful of the houses are still rented (from a private landlord), the remainder being owner-occupied.

THE GARDEN SUBURB INSTITUTE TO THE OLIVE MOUNT CUTTING

Continue walking along Thingwall Road, then stop at the next road junction, which is Fieldway. The traffic lights in the distance mark the Queens Drive crossroads. It was the existence of Queens Drive which helped determine the site of the Garden Suburb, for it was assumed that trams would one day run along it to take the residents to work. In fact the area originally earmarked for development straddled the Drive, and extended almost as far as Broad Green railway station.

[Masthead of 'The Thingwallian', 1914, featuring the houses in Fieldway]

This stretch of Queens Drive - 'Liverpool's circumferential boulevard' as it was described by its designer John Brodie - opened in 1910, just as the development of the Garden Suburb was starting. From the start it was a dual carriageway road, for Brodie - Liverpool's City Engineer from 1898 to 1926 - was exceptionally far-sighted and anticipated the growth of motor traffic. Trams never did run along it, however, and for many years residents of the Suburb had to rely on trains from Broad Green or trams from the Picton Clock.

Turn left into Fieldway, and walk towards the privet hedge which is visible straight ahead. This hedge encloses Fieldway Green, the centrepiece of Sutcliffe's portion of the Garden Suburb. The houses form a quadrangle facing on to the green, creating the sense of community which was the constant aim of Garden City and Garden Suburb designers. Walk to the left, alongside the perimeter hedge, until you reach the gap which gives access to the grassed area.

The houses in Fieldway were built in 1913, and Fieldway Green - which Sutcliffe had originally envisaged as the site of tennis courts - was the scene of summer Rose Queen Festivals for several years afterwards. In July 1914 - on the day of the Institute stone-laying - it was the venue for a Pageant depicting English village life through the ages. As the Liverpool Daily Post reported: "In the last scene of all the lesson of the display was given. Life in a monotonous street of the ordinary suburban type was shown in contrast with the life of a garden suburb". The latter was, no doubt, acted out by the most rosy-cheeked of the local children!

[The first Summer Festival on Fieldway Green, 1913]

It was the 'humdrum existence' of most city residents - separated from their neighbours by tall brick walls - which inspired the designers of Garden Suburbs. "All gardens bordered by mature hedges; no ugly wooden fences" was still the proud boast when the houses were offered for sale to individuals in the 1930s.

Wavertree Garden Suburb was made a Conservation Area in 1971, and it is the aim of the City Planning Department to retain its character as far as possible. Garden walls and fences, as well as UPVC and 'picture' windows, are - in theory at least - outlawed.

Continue walking round the perimeter of the Green. The growth of car ownership among Suburb residents was something not anticipated by the original designers; a few houses were provided with cycle sheds, but that was all. Pass through the archway at the end, under the balcony which provided the VIPs with a grandstand view of the festivities on the Green. Then continue along the footpath which leads through to Heywood Road. (The ancient Childwall Brook runs beneath this path, which was one reason for the gap in the terrace at this point).

Heywood Road marks the northern boundary of the L.G.S.T. estate. The semi-detached villas on the other side of the road were built in the 1880s, long before the Garden Suburb was even contemplated. Turn left and walk towards the parade of shops, crossing over when you reach the curtain factory (originally a co-operative retail store).

The address of the shops is Wavertree Nook Road, which makes an S-bend at this point. The original Wavertree Nook - 'nook' meaning a corner - was a cluster of cottages a little further along the road to the right, in the north-easternmost corner of the old

Township of Wavertree. The name survives on modern Ordnance Survey maps and the Liverpool A to Z, though the hamlet was obliterated by Council housing development over seventy years ago.

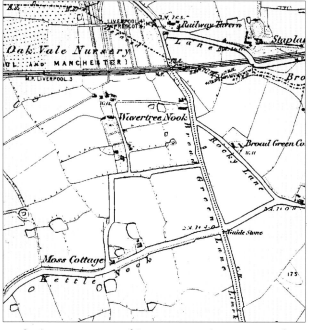

[Ordnance Survey map of the Wavertree Nook area, circa 1849]

The lack of planned shops was among the few grievances of the early Garden Suburb settlers. It was left to the Toxteth Co-operative Provident Society to establish this facility - outside the official boundaries of the Suburb - in September 1914.

Walk on past the shops and turn right into Beechtree Road. Olivetree Road, across the way, is a cul-de-sac privately developed in the 1920s, but the bulk of the housing in this area was built by Liverpool City Council. Beechtree Road and Waldgrave Road, which you will shortly reach, form part of the Edge Lane Drive housing estate, laid out following the Housing &

Town Planning Act of 1919. This Act of Parliament had been inspired by Raymond Unwin, and Liverpool - with its enormous problem of slum housing and overcrowding - was one of the first cities in the country to take advantage of its subsidy provisions.

The City Council had estimated, in 1919, that 15,000 new houses were needed to alleviate the shortage of homes in Liverpool. A total of over 1,200 acres were acquired, and by 1923 over 5,000 houses had been built by the Council. The Edge Lane Drive estate comprised almost 800 houses, the scheme including the extension of Edge Lane as one of John Brodie's new dual carriageway roads and electric tram routes.

The influence of the Garden Suburb movement on the layout of this early Council estate is obvious. The houses are in short terraces, with gardens back and front and grass verges lining the streets. There were also, originally, long avenues of roadside trees, but unfortunately they were all of one species and succumbed to Dutch Elm Disease in the 1970s.

Standardisation of tree-planting and standardisation of house design were two aspects in which the example of the pre-war Garden Suburb was not followed, but obviously money was short and time was of the essence. In fact the City Council did not employ an architect at this time - Lancelot Keay was not appointed until 1925 - and house design was entrusted to a Surveyor, Frederick Badger, who became the city's Director of Housing in 1919.

Walk along Beechtree Road, cross over and then turn left into Waldgrave Road at the far end. The houses here were originally built in the 1920s, and some of them have had to be reconstructed in recent years

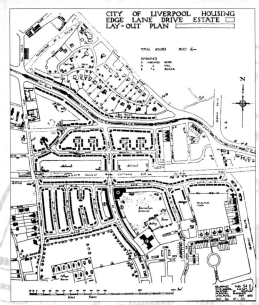

[Layout plan of the Edge Lane Drive housing estate, 1922]

owing to structural failure. Northway Primary School - which you will soon reach on the left-hand side - opened (as the Northway Council School) in 1927. That was a benefit for the residents of the Garden Suburb, for going to school had previously involved a long trek to Wavertree village or even to Smithdown Road, except for the few who attended 'temporary' classes at the Institute.

Both Mr Badger and Mr Brodie, the City Engineer, were keen on experimenting with new methods of house construction. (A brochure published in 1923 boasted that fourteen different methods of construction had so far been adopted by the Council). Looking to the left and right at the Northway crossroads you can see small groups of semis built out of concrete blocks. Cross Waldgrave Road at this point, then cross Northway and continue walking along Waldgrave Road as it climbs towards the top of Olive Mount.

At the top of the hill, turn right into Mill Lane. A few yards further on you will reach a bridge which - when first constructed in 1830 - gave sightseers a grandstand view of one of the engineering wonders of Britain: the Olive Mount Railway Cutting.

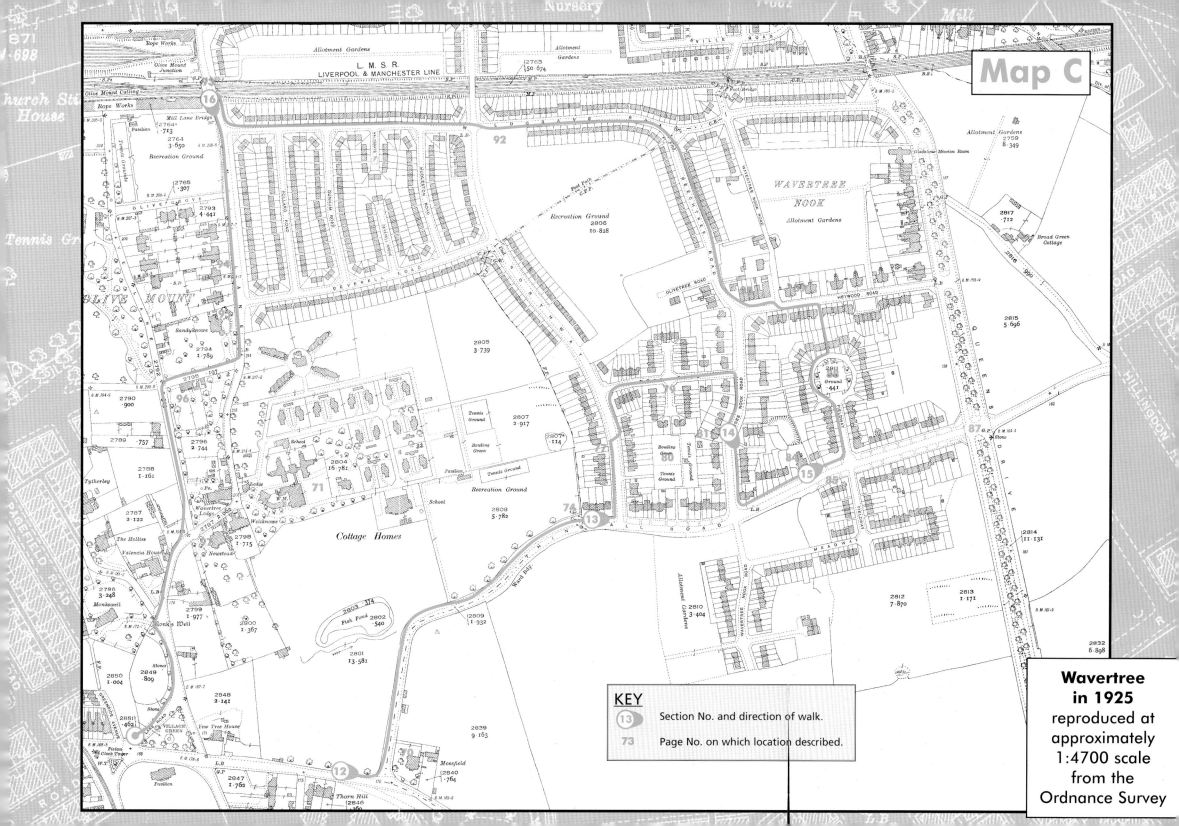

Map C

Wavertree
in 1925
reproduced at
approximately
1:4700 scale
from the
Ordnance Survey

KEY

(13) Section No. and direction of walk.

73 Page No. on which location described.

THE OLIVE MOUNT CUTTING TO THE PICTON CLOCK

Looking over the right-hand parapet wall of the bridge, you can see the sandstone chasm which carries

the Liverpool & Manchester Railway towards Broad Green and beyond. Cross Mill Lane, with care, and look over the other parapet of the bridge towards the city centre. In 1830, when the line opened as the world's first passenger railway, the cutting must have looked even more spectacular, for it was only half the present width.

The Rocket in the Olive Mount Cutting, 1830

George Stephenson, the railway's engineer, had hoped to avoid such problems by routeing the line further north. However, objections from the Earls of Derby and Sefton forced him to adopt this approach to Liverpool, through a cutting nearly two miles long and up to 70 feet deep. The work was carried out by an army of navvies, with the help of horses and explosives but very few mechanical aids. On its completion, the cutting was regarded as one of the wonders of the age, and people from Liverpool and elsewhere would travel to the Mill

Lane bridge to gaze down upon the 'Rocket' and its fellow locomotives.

The growth of rail traffic was such that, before long, the cutting was increased in width from two to four tracks. Some of the extracted stone was made available for local building work, rather than simply being used to enlarge the Roby embankment.

In the middle distance - in front of the Roman Catholic cathedral's distinctive silhouette - are the buildings and landscaping of the Wavertree Technology Park, which was created from 1983 onwards on the site of another 'wonder of the railways': the Edge Hill Gridirons, employing 'Harry Footner's system of sidings for marshalling trains by gravitation'. (The National Railway Museum in York has a model of the sidings in their original form).

Now walk back along Mill Lane, passing the end of Waldgrave Road on the opposite side. Cross the end of Birch Grove and Olive Grove and, a few yards further on, you will come to a row of eight very large semi-detached houses dating from the 1840s and '50s. These are 'Olive Mount Villas', and all of them are Listed Buildings.

This location - right on the top of Olive Mount, one of the highest points in the vicinity of Liverpool - was obviously regarded as a prestigious place to live in Victorian times. The four which had been completed at the time of the 1851 Census were occupied by two merchants (one born in Liverpool, the other in Scotland), an ironmonger (born in Birmingham) and a contractor (born in Dorset). The contractor was John Bowers, who lived at the present-day No.1 Olive Mount Villas - then called 'Greenfield House' - with his wife, mother-in-law, three grown-up daughters but - unusually - no servants. The birthplaces of his daughters - Caroline (aged 28) born in Kent, Selina (25) born in Middlesex and Mary Ann (20) born in Liverpool - indicate the way in which the family had moved around the country before settling in Wavertree.

Continue along Mill Lane until you are standing opposite the entrance to 'Mount Royal', a housing estate built in the 1990s on the site of the Olive Mount Childrens Hospital. The street names on this estate - Swan Crescent, Crossley Drive and Hollins Close - were suggested by the Wavertree Society, and commemorate former owners of the old Olive Mount mansion.

[Sandy Knowe]

The large red sandstone house behind the wall to your right is called 'Sandy Knowe'. The conversion and extension of this early-Victorian house to form sheltered flats was carried out by Merseyside Improved Houses in 1975. Prior to that, the house had been used as an Independent Methodist church, but originally it was the home of Sir James Picton. Knighted in 1881 by Queen Victoria, Sir James died here at Sandy Knowe in 1889.

James Allanson Picton - architect, surveyor, historian and promoter of public libraries - had designed the house himself in 1847, having deliberately chosen the very highest point of Olive Mount: 215 feet above sea level. The son of a builder, he had been born in Highfield Street, off Tithebarn Street in Liverpool, in 1805, but later lived in Warren Street (near Brownlow Hill) before moving to Laurel Road (off Edge Lane) and finally to this house in Wavertree.

Picton was a seasoned traveller, being in the habit of touring different parts of Britain and Europe each summer. He was also a literary scholar, and named his new house after the farm where Sir Walter Scott was brought up, in the Scottish border country . In fact there is a distinct similarity between Sandy Knowe, here in Mill Lane, and Smailholm Tower - an old border fortress - which stands on a rocky outcrop by Sandyknowe Farm, near Kelso. The polygonal sandstone extension - displaying the family arms - was built to house Picton's own private library.

Turn right from Mill Lane into Long Lane, walking on a remnant of the old cobbled surface alongside the Sandy Knowe boundary wall. Cross over by the Liverpool Masonic Bowling Club. This building was originally 'Olivebank Cottage', where Dr Henry Park - the famous Liverpool surgeon who had attended the birth of William Gladstone - is reputed to have lived in retirement. The 1851 Census recorded his daughters - Elizabeth aged 68 and Charlotte aged 64, described as 'landed proprietors and fund holders' - together with their niece and two 'house servants'. The two servants had both been born in the Isle of Man.

Turn left at the crossroads into Olive Lane. A hundred yards along, on the right-hand side, are two large and very distinctive brick-fronted Victorian houses, built in the

1850s. At the 1861 Census the first of these (which has the name Selside on the gate-pier) was home to Thomas Carter, a 'window-blind manufacturer employing 5 men and 2 boys'. The second (Highfield) was the home of John Lewis, a 'fringe manufacturer'. Successive editions of Gore's Directory indicate that these two families remained in residence for many years afterwards.

After a few more yards Olive Lane merges with Mill Lane. Cross the end of Valencia Road, a 1930s cul-de-sac built on the site of Valencia House. This was - in the late nineteenth century - the home of William M'George, a fruit broker: hence, presumably, the name Valencia.

Stop and look across the main road, towards Old Mill Lane: the original course of Mill Lane until it was straightened and widened in the late 1920s to carry electric trams. The impressive, stuccoed building with the castellated turret is 'Newstead', now a Roman Catholic residential home but originally a private house. In 1881 it was the home of Joseph Smith, an iron merchant, who lived there with his wife, three small children and no less than eight domestic servants. The Census records that both he and his wife (aged 48 and 39 respectively) had been born in Liverpool, but the servants were drawn from a wide area: a laundry-maid from Wavertree, a nurse and under-nurse from Liverpool, a kitchen-maid from Chester, a maid from St Asaph, and two housemaids from Ruabon.

In 1890 Mr Smith sent a letter of protest to the Wavertree Local Board of Health, which was constantly striving to improve the amenities of the district:

"My dear Sir, I must ask the Board not to put a seat opposite my field. The one put by the lake is a nuisance, roughs from the Swan use it and I was told by one who passed it a few nights back that the language of those using it made him shudder. Besides the footpath is not wide enough, anyone sitting on it with his legs out would compel all passengers to walk into the road...

"P.S. Respectable people do not sit on such from ten to 11 at night."

A century later, perhaps similar views would be expressed! Certainly, to judge from the Minute Books of the Local Board, the 'good old days' in Wavertree were by no means free from controversy and the problems which we think of as modern.

You are now on the final stretch of a walk which has covered five miles and three thousand years of Wavertree's history! For too long the area's heritage has been taken for granted, and little by little the features which make it such an interesting part of Liverpool have been eroded. Walk on past the Monks Well - source of water for centuries past, and of legend and folklore for generations to come - which was almost lost in the 1930s. Walk on past the site of Wavertree Lake, the filling-in of which, seventy years ago, is still regretted by many local residents. Walk on past the Lock-up, which was earmarked for demolition in the 1860s.

Complete your tour by returning to the Picton Clock Tower, which has presided over the High Street for over a hundred years. The changes witnessed by the Clock Tower have been immense, but the character of Wavertree as a 'village in the city' is still more or less intact. Whether the same will be true a century from now, only time will tell. One thing is certain: if the current interest in local history can be translated into action - into conservation and restoration of the best things from the past - then Wavertree's future is looking brighter now than it has done for a long while.

We hope you have enjoyed the walk!

FURTHER READING

Barker, Eddie:
In and Around Broad Green (1991)

Gould, Colin:
A Pictorial History of Wavertree (1983)

Healey, Peter (ed.):
The Liverpool Blue Coat School Past and Present (1995)

Hoult, James:
West Derby, Old Swan and Wavertree (1913)

Pevsner, Nikolaus:
The Buildings of England - South Lancashire (1969)

Royden, Michael:
Pioneers and Perseverance - A History of the Royal School for the Blind (1991)

Sands, Nigel:
Wavertree (1976)

Schroeder, James:
The Life and Times of Wavertree Parish Church of the Holy Trinity (1994)

SOURCE MATERIAL

All the following are available for consultation in the Liverpool Record Office (Local Studies Library), William Brown Street, Liverpool:

Census returns
(1841-1891)

Wavertree Local Board of Health minute books *(1851-1895)*

Maps and plans
(Leather's 1836, Tithe Award 1846, Ordnance Survey six inch 1851, Ordnance Survey 1:2500 1893, 1908 and 1927)

Street directories
(Gore's Liverpool, later Kelly's)

INDEX

ABOUT THE SOCIETY

Founded in 1977, the Wavertree Society aims to improve local amenities and to protect the local environment and architectural heritage, especially within the Wavertree Village and Wavertree Garden Suburb Conservation Areas. Registered with the Civic Trust. Charity Registration No.1004259.

If you LIVE in, WORK in or just have an INTEREST in the Wavertree area ... Past, Present and Future ... WHY NOT JOIN US?

The more members we have, the more influential we can hope to be. For current subscription rates and a sample Newsletter, write to

**The Wavertree Society,
P.O. Box 100,
Wavertree,
Liverpool L15 5DQ.**